Second Advent in Approach

— A Timeline Study —

B. Smith

Second Advent in Approach: A Timeline Study
B. Smith
ISBN 978-1-77342-093-6

Produced and Published by IndieBookLauncher.com
www.IndieBookLauncher.com
Editing: Nassau Hedron
Cover Design: Saul Bottcher
Interior Design and Typesetting: Saul Bottcher

The body text of this book is set in Adobe Minion.

"Big thanks to Saul and Nas at IndieBookLauncher for making this project happen. They're absolutely the best! The Indie spirit lives on."
—B. Smith

Notice of Rights
Copyright 2019 B. Smith, all rights reserved.
No part of this book may be reproduced or stored in part or in whole via physical copy, audio recording, electronic or digital formats.

Blood Moon image by Wikimedia Commons user Andrey73RUS. Image of Bas-relief on wall of Temple of Edfu, Egypt by Olaf Tausch. Crown of Lower Egypt (Deshret) and Crown of Upper Egypt (Hedjet) images by Käyttäjä:kompak. Double Crown (Pschent) image by Jeff Dahl. New Moon image by NASA Goddard Space Flight Center. Annular Solar Eclipse image by Wikimedia Common user Smrgeog. Total Solar Eclipse image by Luc Viatour.

Images used with permission.

CONTENTS

Foreword 5
1: Podiums 9
2: Y2K Jitters 18
3: The 2012 Mayan Doomsday
   Prediction vs. God 26
4: Wise Men Saw His Star 36
5: About Heavenly Signs 46
6: Anyone Want a Good Used . . . Calendar? 68
7: What's Up With The Sevens? 75
8: No Man Knows The Day or The Hour 81
9: Daniel's Prophesy of The Seventy Weeks 94
10: Moses in Egypt:
    Sub-Timeframe Analysis 114
11: Correlation Between the Red Sea
    Crossing and The Rapture 132
12: The Miracle of The Rapture 138
13: Rapture Found in Revelation 12 168
14: The Rapture is Not The First Resurrection .. 173
15: Rapture Call Audio Characteristics 178
16: Do You See What I See? 185
17: Guidelines for the Timeline Chart 190
18: The Future Beyond the Second Advent 209
In Closing 215
Addendum 217

Foreword

This book is based on my own personal experiences and research I have done after the year 2000.

It incorporates a study of prophetic and historical texts from both the Old and New Testaments of the Bible.

It also incorporates a study of previously published materials from other sources (listed below) that have been thoroughly researched and backed up with factual data. These various sources helped me to look at the topic of the Second Advent from different angles.

The story evolved over the years as more and more information became available.

My interest in this subject was originally born of a curiosity about comments made by co-workers regarding a possible apocalypse immediately following the year 2000, also known as Y2K. Their concerns were mainly derived from writings found in the Book of Revelation.

An undercurrent of nervous anticipation seemed to be gripping the population.

The passing of the year 2000 did not bring an apocalypse, the Great Tribulation or the Second Advent. However, I was intrigued enough to keep my ears to the ground for further news.

As time passed and more information on the subject became available, the blurry matter of a future apocalyptic event became more focused and eventually revealed itself to be a clear target.

My target is a unique time-span of several years that are currently in progress now, in our present, twenty-first century. It's this particular seven-year period that has serious apocalyptic implications because it seems to fit well into the Book of Revelation. I'm talking about the prophet Daniel's seventieth week, a seven-year period.

My book and timeline chart uses the most obviously supportive Biblical texts, supportive astronomical data, the Biblical calendar system, and other information that makes the case for proposing (charting) the location of Daniel's seventieth week on a timeline.

The timeline chart suggests major prophetic events situated at the start, the middle and at the end of Daniel's seventieth week.

The first of these events is a "sign" type event of an astronomical nature that signals the beginning of Daniel's seventieth week (the seven-year period).

The second of these three events is commonly known as the "Rapture" or its original Greek linguistic counterpart, "harpazo."

The third of these three events is commonly known as the "Second Advent of Jesus Christ Messiah."

As some of the information in this book explores certain prophetic future events that cannot be explained as being anything other than wholly miraculous, no attempt has been made to change the miraculous nature as originally described.

If the context of a portion of this study falls within the realm of the supernatural, then it is simply acknowledged as just that.

Allegorical substitution is also avoided.

Some of my homegrown humor is included for free.

The information in this book is geared towards people who are interested in the ancient prophetic texts that are part of the Old and New Testaments of the Bible. It's also for those people who are interested in the science of astronomy.

Another group that would probably find this book interesting are those who are interested in archeology. Part of what substantiates so many of the stories in the Old Testament is the research done by archeologists.

In my opinion, the trail of evidence works in this way: if the archeology proves the stories in the Bible are factual, and it always does, then those facts provide a solid foundation for even more excavating and detailed study.

In my case, I'm not interested in digging up the ground to find what's underneath. I'm interested in digging Biblical, celestial, and historical data to find an elusive time span of seven years called Daniel's seventieth week.

This study acknowledges the excellent research and published materials by the following wonderful people:

Rick Larson
Mark Biltz
Jonathan Kahn

L.A. Marzulli
Richard Shaw
Gil Broussard
Daniel Matson
Jose Escamilla
The Apostle John
The Apostle Paul
The Apostle Matthew
Daniel
Isaiah
Ezekiel
Moses
Job
Joel
Zechariah
Galileo Galilei
Johannes Kepler
Sir Isaac Newton
The good folks at Wikipedia

The conclusions made at the end of this book may seem a bit startling. Please fasten your seatbelts.

1

Podiums

Regarding assorted apocalyptic warnings and the various responses to them, you may have heard something similar to these next few lines.

- Who wants to listen to another apocalyptic warning from some guy on his little podium, shaking his fist in the air and screaming about doom and judgment?
- What's the point in someone repeatedly crying wolf when it's obvious that after all these decades there is no wolf?
- We're all busy with living, working, family, kids, paying the bills, shopping, dining, traveling, web surfing and entertainment. Life has enough problems as it is and we don't need any fearmongers.

These three responses are tops on the short list of reasons that casually dismiss any kind of apocalyptic warning that may pop up from time to time.

But there seems to be something about this message that continues to resonate with a lot of people. It just won't go away quietly and stay away.

The recent expansion of various Christian broadcast networks on radio, TV and the Internet provide for international coverage of this particular topic. There's an attentive audience tuning in from practically every continent.

But they're not alone in the broadcast of this message.

For decades the *entertainment* industry (Hollywood) has picked up on the message and run with it. They've chosen to take advantage of this same subject matter and they've produced countless films on it, haven't they? They have repeatedly produced a parade of cataclysmic end-of-times disaster films. After all, this stuff makes them a lot of money.

Among the many movies based on an "apocalyptic doom" theme there was a movie made that was actually titled *Armageddon*. Gee-whiz! How'd that happen? You mean to tell me that the movie biz has engaged in fear mongering?! Sure looks that way doesn't it?

Armageddon. That's an unusual word isn't it? So exactly where did some desperate little screenwriter in Hollywood find such an obscure word like Armageddon?

That's right! They looked it up and found it in the Bible! You really can't get much more blatant than that, can you?

Looks like the Hollywood crowd has their own podium thing going on, doesn't it? Though they could care less about anything Biblical, they've inadvertently been spreading an apocalyptic warning which actually has its roots in Biblical prophecy.

And you'd probably be correct if you thought that a

small percentage of the audiences for these films retain a tiny bit of prophetic doom syndrome long after the film has run its course.

But let me ask you a question.

Between the folks on their lower budget Christian podium and the Hollywood folks on their bigger budget worldly podium, whose podium is more credible?

The folks on the lower budget podium generally get their information on this particular subject from the Bible in the Book of Revelation (just like Hollywood did) and they're genuinely concerned for humanity. They typically have good intentions and a sincere heart. The warning is proclaimed hoping that some people will take it seriously and be saved. That's a straightforward motive that makes for a fairly credible podium. Just be aware that there are also some hucksters out there on podiums too. Be careful.

Now let's take a look at the world's podium.

The movie industry's podium is huge, extremely powerful and far-reaching. But it's primarily concerned with utilizing subject matter for the purpose of making money, not truly informing. That's why the distortions and contortions of the subject matter are amplified to such a high degree. Their product has to be very entertaining for their target audience to watch (buy) it. And they spend a ton of money to promote it to their target audience too. It's always big on flash but usually weak on facts.

So which podium is better?

To the person with a discerning spirit or anyone with

half a clue, the answer is clear. The lower budget Christian podium is generally the better of the two choices. It usually offers a consistent and reliable discourse.

And after all, would you really want to get a vital end-times warning message that's been put though a cinematography production mill and fine-tuned with spin?

So we've now completed a brief review of the two distinctive presentation styles and methods.

Now let's move on to the more important issue of this alleged end-of-the-world "wolf" that's supposed to arrive on the scene some day. If the subject is as serious as predicted and the wolf actually has sharp teeth, then the effort to find out more details needs to be every bit as serious and sharp.

Don't forget though: regardless of who, how, or where the warnings of doom and judgment come from, it needs to be clearly understood that all this stuff is only preliminary to something else that follows. That "something else", which often gets left out of the picture, just happens to be the Second Advent of Christ Messiah.

What, in the way of new valuable "tangible" information, could be useful for learning more about this important subject? How can some truly applicable *data* be found that will provide meaningful insight? How can we push aside the rhetoric and reruns and arrive at a place where we can say that we truly have a better understand of the situation?

Answer:

- How about some meticulous research?

- How about some research that is not loud or flashy and doesn't require any music playing in the background?

- How about some research that simply puts the information out there without any pretense or spin?

Meticulous solid research is what this book brings to the apocalyptic arena.

I can't claim to be an established or well-known scholar in this arena. I'm not part of any academic association and I'm not an expositor in any public forum.

But I can confidently say that I've built a good case for my timeline study. And I can state that my abilities in logic, pattern recognition, analytics and troubleshooting are absolutely rock solid. These skills, though not typically used in theology, are very handy when it comes to figuring out deep and/or complex matters.

And besides, God gave me these special abilities to put them to good use and not let them collect dust. The way I see it, God created the metal and He created the pedal. So with that in mind, it's my job to put the pedal to the metal and move out onto the track.

The researcher (me) had to first come to the realization (reality) that the factors in play in this study are literal and not figurative. A knowledge base or launching pad of sorts was the result.

I've used excerpts from chapters 4, 5 and 6 to illustrate this. These factors are elaborated in much greater detail within each individual chapter. If you can get hold of these three concepts and let them settle into place then you'll have a good baseline from which to move forward.

✳

Realizing the importance of God's predetermined **astronomical timing framework**. An excerpt from Chapter 4:

The timing of the occurrences of the celestial events show a definite correlation to the events pertaining to the actual birth and death of Jesus Christ Messiah on earth at his First Advent. It's so obvious you can't miss it.

To me, this "timing" aspect had to have been an actual "design" element at the conceptualization stage and subsequent formation of everything that is described in Genesis 1. It would also naturally carry through to the end of Revelation.

The constellation symbolism is remarkable in itself. But when the idea of an actual timing framework for the entire story is understood, it's reasonable to conclude that the framework would include important signal type events that are placed or scheduled at strategic points.

When I understood this, I thought there was a high probability that this same timing framework would not only mark the First Advent but would also certainly have to apply to the future Second Advent.

Could this timing framework include certain star-oriented "threshold markers" or signal type events that may have presented themselves in our modern age?

*

Realizing the importance of God's **divinely appointed scheduling**. An excerpt from Chapter 5:

Genesis 1:14 says . . . "And God said let there be lights in the firmament of heaven to divide the day from the night and let them be for signs and for seasons and for days and years."

The lights are planets and stars. They serve a definite function as God intended.

Here's an interesting note about the English word "seasons" in the verse. The Hebrew word for "seasons" is "moad" and it literally means "appointments". So the correct translation should be appointments, not seasons.

That being the case, the true interpretation of that part of the verse says that the stars and planets function to **sign** (signal) when **appointments** are to happen.

The use of these objects is obviously far beyond any human capability, and yet the audience that God has specifically intended for them is . . . mankind.

This brings up a couple very important questions.

What do these appointments portend for the human race? How do we recognize and understand signals?

*

Realizing the importance of God's **historical legacy calendar system**. An excerpt from chapter 6:

Back to Y2K. If Y2K (year 2000) had everyone on edge due to its supposedly ominous "time's up doom's here" reputation, why did it not produce anything ominous as far a literal event?

Answer: Because the year 2000 is not synchronized to the calendar system for which the ominous future event was planned.

It seems that the prophetic relevance of the Y2K threshold, in terms of its location on our current Gregorian calendar, is completely lost.

Why is that?

Answer: It started with a man in ancient Rome named Julius who decided he wanted his own "standardized" calendar system. A guy with that much arrogance and power gets to have his way. Besides, the glory of Rome knew no limitations.

The Julian calendar is solar-based and it works based on the one year (365 days, 5 hours, 48 minutes to be exact) that it takes for the Earth to complete a full orbit around the sun. He got some help in devising the new system from an Alexandrian astronomer named Sosigenes.

The system that was in place prior to that, the Roman calendar, was a more complex lunar-based system utilizing moon-phase orientation that required regular adjustments. This was done to maintain synchronization with the equinox and solstice cycles. It worked for the most part and time marched on.

Regarding leap years, the Julian system determined that one should fall every fourth year. A leap day was added in the fourth year in the month of February. However, this calculation was incorrect in that it was inserting too many leaps. What this did was throw the timing of the established charted astronomical events "off sync" with the major religious holidays like Easter which follows Passover.

Passover historically syncs up with the first full moon after the vernal equinox.

Did you catch that?

Let me rephrase it in a few different ways. As a result of this calendar modification, a very important religious holiday called "Easter" (right after Passover) was offset or displaced from a significant astronomical association. The astronomical sign value of this special event was basically removed from sight. The celestial storyboard got an unwelcome paint job. Interesting, isn't it?

*

The excerpts above formed the foundational building blocks that allowed me press onward in my research on the subject of prophetic end times.

I was confident that my foundation was solid and level. So I decided to put a podium on it. ☺

2
Y2K Jitters

It was early December of 1999 and I was employed in the fast-paced telecommunications industry, at a Competitive Local Exchange Carrier (CLEC) to be specific. The 1996 Telecom Act that was passed opened up this industry to competition, and we were a part of that new trend.

I suppose that the new technology that was born out of the R&D sector in Silicon Valley was looking for an opportunity to flex its muscles. The telecom industry was totally monopolized, and some tech-savvy people wanted a piece of the action.

We were doing some serious telecom and data stuff that Wall Street liked, so they were throwing a lot of money our way. I was in an engineering group that worked with fiber optic network expansion into commercial areas.

The work was interesting and we were on the cutting edge of this new electronic digital fiber-optic frontier. Silicon Valley in California was a great place to hang out.

Put the glass in. Take the money out. That was the plan.

The technology was good.

The money was good.

The perks were good.

The engineering teams were good.
The technicians were good.
The equipment vendors were great.
The general clerical staff was ok.
The sales team was . . . a sales team.
The receptionist was . . . eventually replaced.

Life was generally pretty good and the future seemed bright. But there was a little problem. There was a software glitch that was rounding the bend and about to arrive at the train station.

Many people were afraid that the glitch might get to the train station but then, instead of arriving smoothly, it would come right off the tracks and destroy the station.

Y2K.

The glitch was due to the software code that controls the yearly increment for computers and computer-controlled systems. This code had the increment formatted as a two digit number: 97, 98, 99 etc. When 99 was completed and 00 was next in line, the matter of how the computers would react to 00 was in question.

The glitch was discovered early enough to engage software code writers to fix the bug, and so the race was on. The code was successfully modified to a four digit format: 1998, 1999 etc. This new revision provided for a smooth transition from 1999 to 2000, to 2001 and beyond.

Computers run a lot of important systems like power plants, municipal water, traffic lights, communications, etc. So fixing this glitch was a very high priority.

Most all systems were fixed and brought up to Y2K compliance by 1998–99.

And guess what? It worked. Very few problems were encountered, critical systems continued to function, and life went on as normal.

But something did happen. Sort of.

After all the systems were modified (patched) successfully and things calmed down, there was still a bit of nail-biting regarding the onset of Y2K.

Perhaps because we were working in the tech sector, with all its amazing fiber-optic-fast-switching-data-packet machinery, we were closer to the core of the issue than most other people. Because of that, we were tuned in a bit better and thus we were more susceptible to being spooked.

There was some strange buzz going around in our office by some people, as Y2K got closer and closer.

But the office buzz didn't seem to be referencing the great progress made by the good folks who rewrote the code. Nor was it about the resilient operational integrity and redundancy of our networks or all the tech staff on standby in case of an emergency outage.

The buzz was oriented towards something quite different. It was a concern about the possibility of a pending doomsday event.

Did I say . . . doomsday?

You heard me right . . . *DOOMSDAY!*

We've all heard of an actual doomsday clock somewhere that is adjusted according to how close the keepers of the clock think our civilization is to an all-out nuclear war, or some other destructive global calamity.

When some country that has nukes becomes very active with its military, and things seem like they could escalate rapidly to code red, the keepers will adjust the arm of the clock closer to the number 12.

Last time I saw some news about this clock they had the arm set at around 11:58 or something. But this scenario has the literal threat of nuclear war as its main premise for the clock's position. The Y2K thing was totally independent of such a "bombs away" scenario. It was more of a tick-tock-tick-tock *"time's up"* event.

So why all the concern about an ordinary thing like the progression of time? How could it act as a catalyst for worldwide catastrophe? Why would this gloomy state of mind appear so suddenly? After all, time has been moving casually forward for centuries and nobody seemed to give it all that much attention.

The news media, in need of ratings, took the opportunity to hype it up. I didn't take the bait. Relax folks. Grab a Snickers bar, sit back, and forget about it.

I was fairly confident that the software glitch would be corrected and these "man made machines" (after all, that's what they are) would continue to operate. And even if they did suffer a software hiccup, our critical computer-controlled infrastructure probably had some fail-over or manual-override capability that would enable them to overcome the hiccup and maintain functionality.

At least I hoped that they would.

But nevertheless, in my opinion, the chatter was generally characterized by an ominous fear of doom. There's no other way to describe the vibe. I heard certain people in the office throw around dialog that included Nostradamus, Revelation, Apocalypse, and the like.

Side note: History has a large catalog of doomsday predictors. One so-called prophetic source by the name of Nostradamus is well known for his apocalyptic predictions. His writings are definitely the stuff of doom. He's even got the correct name for proclaiming doom too: Nostra-*damn*-us! How about that!

A couple people of a religious creed would postulate their assorted doomsday theories with undertones of divine judgment.

But break room conversations never spelled out what the doomsday *main* event would actually be. They would suggest massive earthquakes, volcanoes, and asteroids, among other natural disasters.

I personally didn't succumb to the fear mongers. But it did give me pause to think about any skeletons that I might have in my closet. Maybe I would do a skeleton inventory, just to be on the safe side. ☺

I know that I definitely did hear something that went like this: "Do you think Y2K will be the start of the apocalypse in Revelation?"

I thought up some possible high-tech type scenarios.

Could it be a crash of computer systems that shuts down the grid for who knows how long? Could worldwide communications networks be interrupted? I even remembered a movie called *Dr. Strangelove* that used the idea of an unusual series of circumstances leading up to a computer center being destroyed, which subsequently triggered a worldwide "doomsday device."

Despite all the chatter, nobody could give any specifics or hard data.

But there's one thing for certain that could be said about the Y2K event, and that was this: the concerns were pointing towards a "time-based threshold" as an indicator for potential doomsday on planet Earth.

As far as timing thresholds go, I have some knowledge of this from within our industry.

The networks have clocking systems that all have to be perfectly synchronized. If the timing slips off sync, then the data moving across the networks starts having trouble. Both data and voice traffic can falter if the slip advances to a certain threshold, and then you've got a big problem. Not doomsday, but big problems.

Would you like to hear some tech dribble about "time division multiplexing"?

No, you say? Ok then, we'll keep moving along.

It's funny how something like the concept of clocking can be hidden in the background, but everything in a network ultimately depends on it. I started thinking about timing as related to cataclysmic world events.

Is there some kind of master clock that's running, and God has it set to trip an alarm at a certain point when "*time is up*"?

I've heard of several instances in the past where certain people took this very seriously and as it turned out, time was *not* up. But I'm not going to bash or ridicule these folks. They were just misinformed.

There was also some fun to be had by people on the airwaves. I recall some local radio station that exploited this nervous condition in the population. They aired a sort of doomsday countdown program leading up to 2000, which featured a weird ominous-sounding voice that did the audible countdown.

I would tune into this radio program quite often just to hear the sound of this synthesized voice counting down because it just was so strange.

There were no commercial breaks or any other interruptions. Just a steady continual countdown. That's it.

I remember the night just before the year 2000 crossover. I was in bed trying to sleep, but I knew that I was going to wake up sometime before midnight and tune in to the countdown broadcast.

60 seconds . . . 50 seconds . . . 40 seconds . . . 30 seconds . . . 20 seconds . . . 10. 9. 8. 7. 6. 5. 4. 3. 2. 1 and . . . silence.

I waited in the darkness, listening for the sounds of emergency sirens going off. Nothing. No explosions. No earthquakes. No emergency broadcasts. No nuthin'.

So I turned the radio off, went to sleep, and snored my way right past Y2K.

The next week at work was uneventful. Y2K came and went without any major hiccups. Planet Earth was still orbiting the sun, and the law of gravity was intact.

But now there was a nagging question stuck in the back of my mind. Is there any legitimate substance to the idea that a timeline parameter could forecast worldwide doom or some kind of divine judgment?

Observation/opinion: The Y2K scare turned out to be just that, a scare. But there's an underlying reason for that 2000 AD mark to have provoked such concern and fear.

It's because there resides within every human a built-in awareness of God. I would add that there also seems to be a subconscious awareness within many people that God owns a stopwatch.

3

The 2012 Mayan Doomsday Prediction Versus God

The decade that followed Y2K was not exactly quiet, albeit there was no single cataclysm of such large scale that it would qualify as worldwide destruction. Nothing happened to invoke a common mood in the global psyche that smacked of Apocalypse.

There was some other *big* stuff going on worthy of comment. Some of that action was in the form of hurricanes, earthquakes, volcanoes, and tsunamis. Other disasters came in the form of the Gulf oil spill, the Fukushima nuclear plant meltdown, and so many more that they all can't be listed.

All these events, though severe, didn't pack anywhere near the amount of punch required to deal a final deathblow to planet Earth. But the bad news just kept coming and is still reported on to this day.

The big earthquakes and quake swarms out west (in California and other states) are definitely on the rise. Yellowstone National Park is experiencing some serious ground shifting due to a buildup of subsurface magma. This is considered to be a super-volcano that's about ready to pop its top anytime now.

The nuclear waste from the Fukushima disaster in Japan is polluting the Pacific Ocean. I feel sorry for all the sea life that unknowingly swims through that toxic junk and then has to suffer the aftereffects.

Speaking of sea junk, I'm hearing more and more stories of sea life showing up dead on beaches all over the world with their bellies full of plastic.

Plastic, plastic, plastic . . . so who else has some plastic deposited in their gut?

For decades, we've been sold beverages in containers made of plastic. It was finally discovered that these containers were actually leaching plastic into the beverages that they contained. Fortunately for us, enough people got hip to that crap and "BPA Free" containers are now available.

If all this stuff isn't enough to turn your stomach, I've even heard that the planet Earth is undergoing a gradual shift in electromagnetic polarity.

All this bad news is indicating an increase in the frequency and intensity of disasters that are making the headlines and getting people's attention. That is, until the next pop culture distraction comes along and then it's quickly forgotten.

And I'm not sure if all these worldwide catastrophes are increasing to the point where we can say we're doomed, but overall it doesn't look very good.

There's another thing, mostly in western society, that's been on the rise since Y2K, and that is the doomsday prepper trend. This emergency preparation mindset concerns itself with a few different crisis-based scenarios, not just the Biblical apocalypse. This trend is very real.

The idea of being prepared for tough times is not new. Food storage, self defense, utility backup systems have been around for decades. And even back in the days of the early pioneers, preparedness wasn't optional. It was pre-planned.

But lately, something has provoked the prepper mindset to take things to the next level. There are bunker systems of varying sizes, survivalist camps on private real estate, and underground rent-a-space facilities. There are even converted, decommissioned, security-staffed missile silos to accommodate those who want that higher level of sophisticated provision and protection.

Did I use the word "protection"? Yes I did.

Protection from what, dare I ask? The answers to this question can range from local to national to international. But this book deals with a singular subject that has global scale implications.

So just what type of post-Y2K prediction did arrive on the scene that actually brought a renewed sense of global doom?

It was 2012, another "time-based threshold" omen.

Oh no! Not again! Would someone please stop this ride

already!

Well, we thought that we were all safe for a while. That is until some archeologist discovered an ancient Mayan relic, and by so doing opened up another can of apocalyptic worms.

The Mayan long count calendar.

There was an awful lot of attention given to the Mayan long count calendar and its doom-and-gloom, 2012, end-of-it-all forecast. The year 2012 was widely viewed as a very good candidate for... *The END!*

The target date called out by the long count calendar was December 21, 2012.

This attention was not totally unfounded either.

The fact of the Mayan's incredible accuracy in matters of time tracking and astronomy is well documented. The long count calendar accurately predicted future solar and lunar eclipses. It also just so happens that Dec 21, 2012 is the exact day of winter solstice in the northern hemisphere.

Some bad news: during the course of the Maya culture, there was the very grisly practice of human sacrifice against their own people going on, as evidenced by the archeological records. The day-to-day, year-to-year existence in such an awful setting must have been nothing less than dreadful.

Their main, central, city temple happened to be adorned by a "snake" motif no less. The snake symbol has traditionally been used in depicting the devil, so it's obvious that the Maya leadership were occult. That's the downside.

But they also surprised modern-day researchers with their advanced knowledge of astronomy and mathematics. That's the unexpected upside.

They had some impressive, highly advanced, astronomy-based correlations incorporated into their architecture. Their labor force produced some city complexes that included the iconic pyramid structure. These structures are not simple to make by any means.

So it must be acknowledged that this culture had advanced knowledge that was evidenced by the high degree of accuracy displayed in the long count calendar. This historical fact does warrant considerable respect.

All of the world's nail-biters were on the edge of their seats again. But the 2012 prediction totally fizzled. The only thing it did was moving the dial up a few notches on the jitter meter.

Was it actually prophetic or not?

Here's something totally off the beaten track that I discovered that seems to offer some insight. People might think that this is nothing more than coincidence. But seeing as how my theory has a prophetic timing aspect that serves as the premise, this particular story really jumped out at me.

There's a very interesting documentary that was done by the late Richard Shaw (Pinlight Productions) called *Torah Codes—End to Darkness* (on DVD) that I watched sometime around 2015-16.

The information on this DVD is truly amazing. The conclusion that can be drawn from this information is beyond amazing.

For those who are not familiar with the Torah, that is the Hebrew name for the five books written by Moses. The Torah is slightly over 3,300 years old.

Richards's documentary tells about the discovery of some amazing information that's hidden (coded) in the Torah. The concept is based in the science of numerology. Numerically based patterns are the key to searching out these codes.

The search is done with computer software (Soft Soft Torah) that runs a search of the entire Torah text for key words of interest and then displays the results. The engine at the heart of the software is a called Equidistant Letter Sequencing (ELS). The "Torah codes" equate to coded information in the Torah that are revealed (exposed) by means of the ELS computer search that is run.

The decoded results are displayed on a graphic-and-text composite table that shows the Torah text field overlaid with the resultant key words. It's further enhanced with a color-coded layout to help in organizing the results.

I had my doubts at first, because I thought it might be borderline mysticism and I refuse to go down that road. Mathematics plus hocus pocus equals hocus pocus.

But it turns out that the Torah Code software has been tested repeatedly and proven to work properly. It produces *accurate results* over and over again, to the point where it can't simply be argued against as mere coincidence.

A variety of topics have had their associated key words run by this program against the Torah text and the resultant information has been shown to relate positively to literal events. In other words, the search generates real "hits."

The ELS results also have the uncanny ability to show up embedded in specific parts (lines of text) of the Torah that are very congruent with the searched topic in terms of the literal context.

It appears that that certain current events that have occurred in our age have already been written about in the Torah, but in a coded form!

I'm sure we could all agree that this is *not* anything that Moses could have done (encoded) himself. It's just way too complex. However, it sure looks to be something that's not too complex for God to have orchestrated.

The conclusion that many have reached (including me) goes like this: the encoded information was sourced by deity and was predetermined to remain hidden, for the most part, until the advent of the computer.

That would mean that the generation designated by God (from ages past) to possess and use the specific tools (computers) to decipher this encoded data (knowledge) was *our* generation.

That's right, the people who are living right now in the twenty-first century.

The 2012 prediction was a topic of interest that eventually found its way to one of the people who use Soft Soft

Torah software to conduct ELS search queries.

In 2008, a Jewish professor named Eliyahu Rips performed an ELS search for the 2012 doomsday prediction in the Torah to see if there was anything tucked away somewhere. Lo and behold, he actually did find coded information about the 2012 event in the Torah, in the book of Exodus 16:26.

But the result table for 2012 revealed an enigma. There was, indeed, an actual event foretold in the table. But there was the presence of the word "butau," which means "cancelled." So this means that a catastrophic event of some kind was initially a "GO," but was then *changed* to "NO GO."

I'm sure everyone who saw this ELS table was wondering what kind of event was supposed to happen. Had there been any pre-2012 research that revealed a potential worldwide natural disaster of some kind? Maybe a close call asteroid? Maybe a tectonic plate shift? Only God knows the answer.

So here's the enigma breakdown:

- A 2012 end-time doom prediction is found on a Mayan stone relic from an archeology investigation and is widely covered in the news.

- 2012 comes and goes with no doomsday.

- All the folks who are camped out in their emergency underground bunkers have to blow out their candles and come back out.

- The dreaded 2012 Mayan doomsday no-show event shows up in a Torah Code search result table, but there's a cancellation notice attached to it.
- The 2012 predicted doomsday event couldn't be just a mere fluke because it's actually mentioned in the Torah in Exodus 16:26 via an ELS search.

Well, stay tuned and don't touch that dial! There might be an explanation for what caused the cancellation of this 2012 doomsday event!

If you're in sync with this book so far, then you'll probably agree that God is sovereign and omniscient concerning all things. This would include the apocalyptic predictions from pagan cultures of the past, or any other future, end-time event scenario that happens to come along.

If an end-time event of global Biblical scale was supposed to happen in 2012 but was called off, what could have happened in 2012 that would have been enough to counteract the initiation of that event?

Who called it off?

Well, maybe instead of doomsday, God gave mercy in the form of a *warning*.

Here's a suggestion for how that warning could have manifested: A bestselling book called *The Harbinger*, by Jonathan Cahn, released in the year of . . . **2012.**

So what's the deal? Here's the deal.

Point 1: Y2K was a "time-based threshold" oriented omen that spoke of "Time's up."

Point 2: 2012 was a "time-based threshold" oriented omen that spoke of "Time's up."

Point 3: We are a civilization that seems to have an inner spiritual awareness or fear of a pending future "Time's up" event.

Question: could there really be a divine stopwatch running on humanity?

4

WISE MEN SAW HIS STAR

After a busy Friday of high-tech telecom engineering and Free Cell, I decided to go home, sink down in the recliner, and watch some television. I normally like to check out the channels that feature historical or scientific documentaries. While clicking on the remote, I happened to stop on a channel that was showing some guy in a library giving a lecture to a small audience.

His name was Rick Larson. He introduced himself as a teacher in his church and a lawyer by profession. He was covering his subject material in a very logical and scientific sort of way, and stated that his spiritual orientation was Christian.

His presentation was on a theory he had about the astronomy pertaining to the star of Bethlehem story. He had his laptop computer running an astronomy program to project his presentation onto a big screen on the back wall.

It was clear that this type of complex research could not have been done, to the degree of accuracy required, without a computer. And as Rick stated in order to emphasize this point, "We can. We have software."

I was really impressed by this because, frankly, I too

am a logical, scientific person of the same faith, and when someone can back up their subject matter with solid facts, verified with technology, I'm right there.

Anyway, further on he was making reference to some ancient texts from the Book of Revelation. This caused me to sit up and pay close attention. It was the verse in Revelation 12 that tells about "a great wonder in Heaven" that the Apostle John saw. I've read this same text before but never understood what it meant.

Rick explained, and showed clearly, that this great wonder in Heaven was actually formed by the constellation Leo with the constellation Virgo below it.

This was the first time that I had ever heard a good explanation for a correlation between a celestial event and an apocalyptic event. In my mind, the extreme nature of the events described in Revelation would imply that this dual constellation appearance would also have extreme importance. It shouldn't be downplayed. It's significant.

I remembered that the Book of Revelation also happened to be the source for some of the Y2K doomsday speak that was going around our office.

Revelation is a difficult book to understand and Rick acknowledged this fact. I've read it many times since the Y2K event.

I discovered a little something that may help readers out there to understand how the progression through Revelation works.

If you read Revelation as a series of overviews instead

of in a straight linear-chronological fashion, it will start to click in.

If you think of each overview as a segment of the entire Revelation that one "flies over" in a circular pattern to view the scenario below, then it will start making sense.

With each completed circular "fly-over", starting at high level (Chapter 1) and gradually progressing to mid and lower levels, we are given different details and different perspectives on the components of the Great Tribulation period.

In continuing the aerial survey, there's a gradual descent to the lower levels where more detailed perspective and eventually the conclusion (landing zone/Second Advent) can be seen. Scofield's notes are very helpful for this study.

But Revelation 12 is a unique departure from the rest of the Bible. It opens up a totally different box, or maybe a "star gate." It tells a story with an astronomical interlace that, in my opinion, bridges the gap between prophesy and astronomy.

More on this later.

Back to my TV. I locked into the channel and started watching. I was totally fascinated. There was a lot of good information. But to comprehend it fully in just one session was impossible.

So I looked him up on the Internet, found his website, and ordered the DVD of his Star of Bethlehem presentation. I needed to watch the whole presentation carefully from start to finish because there was so much material covered.

The entire presentation turned out to be a very well-researched and comprehensive study of the astronomy that was used by the wise men who traveled to Bethlehem and found the baby Jesus Christ Messiah.

This astronomy, rediscovered and presented by Rick, is undoubtedly a real factor (knowledge) that was understood and used by the wise men from the east who found Jesus in the town Bethlehem, Israel.

And he was very careful to point out that they were using the science of "astronomy" and not the diluted con game version known as "astrology."

The "bright star" was actually was formed by conjunctions involving Jupiter with other planets (Venus and Regulus) that, by virtue of their closeness, produced a much greater light output. This phenomenon is what gave the events prophetic "sign value."

Jupiter is the King planet. Venus is the Mother planet. Regulus is the King star. These are the essential celestial players that formed the signs that sent the message.

The bright star conjunctions (signs) occurred within constellations that have an obvious association with the nation of Israel and ultimately Christ Messiah himself.

The additional involvement of "Blood Moons," or what is commonly known today as Total Lunar Eclipses, reinforced the importance of astronomy as applied to the overall prophetic context.

Also, the combined timing and symbolism of all these events was shown to be much too perfect and relevant to be anything other than God's handiwork.

I finally had learned something tangible pertaining to the Star of Bethlehem and the surrounding history. And it was backed up with accurate data. It was very refreshing, because it was a totally hype-free infusion of new knowledge. I immediately connected this to Daniel 12:4: "Many shall run to and fro and **knowledge shall be increased**." This made a big impact on me.

I've personally witnessed the amazing advancement in knowledge within the tech sector because it's always been my stock in trade. It's what I do.

Take the humble calculator for example. It was a big leap forward. Push some buttons and get a perfect result. It's much faster than math with paper and pencil. The improvement in speed opens up new possibilities. That's a fact. But why now?

Why did the last seventy-five-plus years produce the most incredible increase in knowledge ever known to mankind? And particularly the last twenty years have produced exponential advances that no one could have ever imagined.

Answer: The computer.

What about the "why now" question with respect to the end-times knowledge increase that's mentioned in Daniel 12:4?

Answer: Why not now?

Let me ask you a couple questions:

1) Are you happy and content with not having to deal with the possibility of living in the prophetic time frame that Daniel warned about?

2) Does the thought of being provoked to take a real hard look at this new end-times astronomy knowledge bother you?

For many people, knowledge is a generally good thing.

But it seems like end-times knowledge is a sort of Pandora's box that most people would rather not open.

The extensive astronomy research that Rick did (with a computer) resulted in important "knowledge" *rediscovered*. The box is now open.

With respect to the traditional Christian knowledge-base catalog, this new type of solid research and in-depth analysis has not made the grade. My guess is that it's a bit too cutting edge, and thus gets displaced with familiar, redundant, programmatic rhetoric. That's a real shame.

There's lots of new evidence available that supports the accounts that are written in the Old and New Testament. A lot of it is from archeology and from the scientific research (cutting edge) that is done to authenticate it. It needs more exposure.

A primary example in this area is the work done by the late Ron Wyatt with his discovery of the Noah's Ark site in 1977. The archeological research was eventually documented on a DVD called "Revealing God's Treasures." I would highly recommend this documentary to anyone.

In the case of Rick Larson, his research is based in astronomy, and the resulting facts are very compelling to say the least. After viewing his research, I was convinced of the reality of the celestial realm being used by God in signaling sacred prophetic events as detailed in the scriptures.

There was more to his research that fascinated me. It was the "precision timing" that is inherent in the celestial system. I was compelled to check it out further. The celestial system does have an intrinsic clock mechanism at work, albeit an extremely large one. I have to stop here briefly to share some amateur astronomer perspective.

This celestial clock doesn't use tiny gears and springs to wind up the mechanism or batteries to power it up. It uses planets and stars.

There's something a bit scary about that concept because it would take a lot of strength to wind up a bunch of planets and stars wouldn't it?

Now add to that initial creative act the business of organizing select groups of celestial stuff (galaxies), starting them into motion, and then distributing them all over the universe. If that's not enough, they also appear in a wide variety of forms and colors. The entire cosmic package combines physics, mathematics, and yes, artistry.

According to what is written in Genesis 1, the designated vantage point (observation deck) for this amazing display is . . . the planet Earth. This is key.

In our own solar system, the planets are moving in perfectly synchronized perpetual motion on invisible elliptical tracks set against a backdrop universe of constellations. There's no oil to change and there are no bearings to grease. The whole solar system just keeps moving along, orderly and quiet.

The word "system" in solar system has implications.

Our solar system is indeed a "system," and that word system implies ... design. The system has placed the Earth at just the perfect distance from the Sun so that it is properly warmed and can sustain life, as well as the cyclical functions of all the ecosystems. There's a sort of balancing act going on.

Fact: sunlight, taken in moderation of course, even helps the human body to produce vitamin D!

The entire system is remarkable in terms of sheer function and practical benefits. This had to be the work of a Creator. There's really no way to dispute this.

For example, take the moon and the way it affects the tides. Ever wonder what the purpose of tides is? Maybe it's a simple matter of swishing the water around a bit in order to keep it fresher. What a concept!

This same swishing effect could also be accomplished by gently shaking up the planet Earth, but then our dinner would fly off the kitchen table onto the floor and everything would be a mess. ☹

Anyway ...

The timing of the occurrences of the celestial events, as detailed by Rick, show a definite correlation to the events pertaining to the actual birth and death of Jesus Christ Messiah on Earth at his First Advent. It's so obvious you can't miss it.

To me, this "timing" aspect had to have been an actual "design" element at the conceptualization stage and subsequent formation of everything that is described in Genesis 1. It would also naturally carry through to the end of Revelation.

The constellation symbolism is remarkable in itself. But when the idea of an actual timing framework for the entire story is understood, it's reasonable to conclude that the framework would include important signal-type events that are placed or scheduled at strategic points.

When I understood this, I thought there was a high probability that this same timing framework would not only mark the First Advent but would also certainly have to apply to the future Second Advent.

Could this timing framework include certain star-oriented "threshold markers," or signal-type events that may have presented themselves in our modern age?

The research in the field of Biblical astronomy may be totally abstract to most people, but it really needs to be given serious consideration.

It certainly opened my eyes to reality of the astronomical factor being essential for a better understanding of Biblical history and the prophetic horizon.

God doesn't want us to be aimlessly stumbling in the dark. The Wise Men observed the stars. We should be doing the same.

There must be some more celestial threshold "markers" out there. There must be more to the story.

5

About Heavenly Signs

The statement by Apostle Paul in Romans 1:20 sets the stage for God's *creation,* giving irrefutable proof of His *existence*. Rom 1:20 says "For the invisible things of him from the creation of the world are clearly seen, being understood by the things that are made, his eternal power and Godhead; so that they are without excuse."

If looking at the wide variety of forms of life on the planet were not enough to convince anyone of creation, then the complexity of the ecosystems that function to support it all should certainly do the trick. This is reasonable. Humans were created by God with the ability to see, think, and reason. That being the case, they would have to be subject to the jurisdiction of Romans 1:20.

Let's look into the words "clearly seen" and "without excuse" and dig a little deeper.

The phrase "clearly seen": It's simply saying that God's creation is viewable to all humans (things that are made) without any obstruction.

The phrase "without excuse"? It's simply saying that the unobstructed view of God's creation by humans makes them 100% accountable for acknowledging the truth of this reality. Problem is, they don't care. And as we all know, you just can't reason with unreasonable people.

Here are a couple of scenarios.

In the terrestrial realm:

- The wide variety of animal and plant life on planet earth staggers the mind.
- The fossil records reveal an even greater pre-existent variety.
- The cyclical geo systems that allow for them to flourish are incredible.
- The beauty and sophistication of the natural landscapes are breathtaking.
- The underlying subsurface mantle and related tectonics inspire awe and fear.
- The availability of natural resources for use by mankind is truly a gift from God.

There's a lot to appreciate in this earthly realm. In the celestial realm: On a night with good visibility, if you're outside and looking up, there's an amazing cosmos that is staring back down at us.

Every time I have this encounter, I wish that I had some kind of fast space transportation so that I could get out there and check it out more closely. I'm talking about really fast. I would only be able to do this on weekends for obvious reasons.

The sparkly lights up above are yelling at me: "Hey you!

Yeah, you down there!"

Maybe you've wondered about this question like I have. What's really out there past the great starry beyond?

There's another nagging question that persists: is heaven really somewhere beyond the stars, and will I get there someday?

I'm quite sure this same question has bothered people since the pre-flood period. I suspect that, centuries later, the scientists Nicholas Copernicus, Isaac Newton, Galileo Galilei, and Johannes Kepler were all bothered by it.

Kepler was a very interesting case in point. His mathematical formulas for charting the movement of the planets and stars were, among other things, used by him to search for the Star of Bethlehem, which was described in the Book of Matthew.

The discoveries made by Copernicus, Newton, Galileo, and Kepler changed how the world viewed the celestial realm. In my opinion, the period in which these men lived (1470's–1720's) was meant (designed?) to bring a new comprehensive "knowledge increase" that was a stepping stone for future astronomical research.

This concentrated 250-year period *somehow* happened to produce some of the greatest scientific minds of that age. These minds *somehow* catapulted the science of astronomy right out of the dark ages into a correct understanding of factual data. Then this celestial knowledge explosion *somehow* happened to dovetail right into the mechanical and industrial revolution. Just a fluke?

Modern astronomy, with modern optical equipment, has produced an incredible catalog of images. The R&D that has been done by NASA over the years has informed many other tech industries. These days the telescopes are much bigger, but the angst for celestial knowledge is still the same.

It seems that every so often there's some news about an astronomical discovery that could indicate the possibility of... *other life forms in outer space!!* Well isn't that amazing! What a shocking epiphany!

Of course there are other life forms out there. God, the angels, the cherubim, the seraphim, and all the saints of the past are out there. And yes, sorry to say it, but there are some demonic angels out there too.

If they had asked me, I could have saved them a lot of time and money.

The celestial realm is something important that God has created for all of us to look at and reflect on. But nowadays, for most people, the terrestrial world offers so many distractions that the celestial is put on the shelf to collect dust.

We can all admit it. Times have changed. Modern day life, especially in western culture, keeps us all very busy. It seems like we're always hurrying to get to our next race. The constant fast pace is never ending.

The technology-based products of this era provide for a level of efficiency that was not previously known. But they also allow for excess leisure time that often gets spent (wasted) on entertainment, social endeavors, and other things.

Unfortunately, it's spiritual awareness that gets offset by distractions that appear on a little screen. The little screen has everyone looking down, not up.

But even though our culture is hopelessly captivated by modern tech distractions, the "things that are made" (Rom 1:20) are *not exempt* from "his eternal power and Godhead." In place of the word "captivated" here, we could just as well say "trapped."

The trap is subtle at first, but, over time, the strength of its grip increases. And it can sadly cause blindness in the eyes of the "things that are made" (people).

Albeit, they're still "without excuse."

For those who are skeptical of the use of the stars and planets by God in expressing Himself to mankind, take a look at the book of Job. God is asking Job questions with regard to His creation, and specifically the constellations.

The line of questioning makes no pretense about who created the universe.

Again, this is astronomy, *not* astrology. Let's take a look at some examples.

Example 1

In Job 38:31, God asks Job a direct question: "Canst thou bind the sweet influences of Pleiades or loose the bands of Orion?"

That's a kind of strange question because it assigns human traits to non-human entities. It also is saying that

God himself has authority over the constellations in that He determines the nature of whatever messages they're sending.

I can't imagine being able to communicate directly with God in the way that Job did, though most of the conversation was God shutting Job down with a lecture.

The dialog pertaining to the celestial assumes that Job fully understood the celestial. But who taught him this stuff in the first place?

I believe that Job and many others of his time recognized the fact that God designed the celestial with beauty, verve, and time-tracking functionality.

Here's a fact. It's been known for centuries that sailors relied on the regularity of the heavenly clockworks for use in navigating the globe. I would suggest that people of former cultures also understood that, as the arms of the clock (planets) move across the face (background of constellations), they convey information.

Ask yourself these questions:

1) Why did God go to the extent of giving specific names to the constellations and communicate this information to humans?

2) Why is the influence of Pleiades described as sweet instead of bitter?

3) Why did God say that Orion is wearing a band (belt) and that it can be loosed?

4) Did Orion have to loosen his belt because he ate too much?

5) The char-grilled Pisces was plentiful but he probably overdid it with that side order of Crab Nebula.

These examples (the first three anyway) demonstrate that God assigns special attributes to His constellations that have their representation in earthly creatures. Why is that?

Answer:

1) It is because God does in fact use his celestial creation to convey messages.

2) The celestial storyboard is not intended to detract from holy prophetic scripture, but is meant to complement and emphasize it.

3) The constellations and planets are set up as a divinely choreographed pictographic storyboard or visual media for the messages.

4) The storyboard has been strategically positioned to envelop the planet Earth for the purpose of observation by its occupants.

5) The observation of the storyboard by the occupants is meant to inform us that the wonder and beauty of the celestial display reflects the Glory of God.

6) The Glory of God and the fact that He would provide all this for us to observe speaks to us to inform us that He cares for us.

7) God's care for us went so far as to send His Only Son to Earth to provide salvation.

8) God's plan for His Son was foretold in His celestial storyboard as described in the Book of Matthew, where

the wise men discerned the star-based signs, followed them, and found Jesus Christ the Messiah in Bethlehem.

The celestial message board worked perfectly as it was designed to do.

Example 2

Genesis 1:14 says "And God said let there be lights in the firmament of heaven to divide the day from the night and let them be for signs and for seasons and for days and years."

The lights are planets and stars. They serve a definite function as God intended.

Here's an interesting note about the English word "seasons" in the verse. The Hebrew word for "seasons" is "moad," and it literally means "appointments." So the correct translation should be appointments, not seasons.

That being the case, the true interpretation of that part of the verse says that the stars and planets function to **sign** (signal) when **appointments** are to happen.

The use of these objects is obviously far beyond any human capability, and yet the audience that God has specifically intended for them is . . . mankind.

This brings up a couple very important questions.

What do these appointments portend for the human race? How do we recognize and understand signals?

Example 3

In Luke 21:25, Jesus adds an extra prophetic imperative that brings the celestial signs into the entire end-time sign group. He said: "And there shall be signs in the sun and in the moon and in the stars."

There should be absolutely no doubt as to what Jesus is referring to in this verse. To make the point, let's take a classic, well-known example.

Over 2000 years ago, some discerning men from somewhere around Babylon knew something very important was happening in the celestial clockworks. They observed the God-given "heavenly signs in the sky" and determined that what was being displayed was a notification of the birth of a new King in Israel.

After they understood the significance, they made a trip to Jerusalem, and their celestial homework led them right to Bethlehem.

They understood that God uses simple bright objects in the sky to convey important information . . . *and they were 100% correct.*

Regarding the star of Bethlehem, after the wise men had arrived in Jerusalem, they explained to Herod the reason for their trip. Matthew 2:2 says, "for we have seen *His* star in the east and are come to worship him."

They knew of a specific bright star within the celestial clockworks that possessed a status so prominent and supreme that it was the one to watch very closely.

But watch . . . *what?*

Watch a sign (bright star = arm of the clockworks) traverse the heavens (constellations = face of the clockworks) to convey information via a storyboard.

For more information on the Star of Bethlehem astronomy, go online and search for Rick Larson and The Star of Bethlehem. The information on this DVD is the definitive key for understanding, not just Biblical astronomy, but the very reason for it.

The people of planet Earth seem to be expecting something to arrive from outer space. Hollywood has exploited this idea for a long time. A famous movie about this subject was the classic *The Day the Earth Stood Still*. There have been many others. But they're all science fiction and meant to entertain.

However, there's a lot of real, certified, celestial observation happening. There are countless ground-based observatories, plus some Hubbles, SOHOs, Grails, and who knows what else floating around out there. Why the expensive launches of the long-range Pioneer and Voyager probes? I'd really like to know the backstory because, after all, my tax money paid for it.

Why were they targeting both of these satellites for a viewpoint aimed towards the constellation of Sagittarius? Was there a special factor in play when the trajectory calculations were made? Is there something about Sagittarius that has sign value?

In other words, was NASA expecting something unusual to poke its head out from behind Sagittarius and say "peek-a-boo"? One really has to wonder what *else* is contained in the photo archive that was produced by these voyages.

To illustrate this point, two movies by filmmaker Jose Escamilla, *Celestial* and *Moon Rising*, feature full-color photography of the moon.

At the time of the making of these films, he was able to obtain (download) available full-color, highly detailed photos of the moon, taken via space reconnaissance missions.

His work revealed some very interesting findings. Certain photos of the lunar surface featured some unusual structures, which prompted some reasonable questions: What is that anomalous thing (an object with symmetrical characteristics) appearing on the surface of the moon? How did it get there?

After the release of Jose's films, the photo archive that once contained nicely detailed imagery with respect to these strange anomalies has been modified. The photos no longer have the fine detail as they once did before and can't be properly studied. By golly, how did that happen?!

The idea of looking up into the heavens for something or someone is not new. But I suspect that the thought of a particular "someone" that left our planet and is said to be returning, may have made some people a bit nervous.

Acts 1:10-11 is noteworthy.

V.10: "And while they looked steadfastly toward heaven as he went up, behold two men stood by them in white apparel;"

V.11: "Which also said, Ye men of Galilee, why stand ye gazing up into heaven? This same Jesus, which is taken up from you into heaven, shall so come in like manner as ye have seen go into heaven."

The good folks over at the space agency seem to be anxious about something ... or someone. Well, they can relax.

If the information in Acts 1:10-11 is indeed true, and Jesus does actually return to Earth, I'm sure that he will make all their anxieties go far, far away.

Let's return to signs.

Please understand that the heavenly signs would most likely have to manifest themselves in the form of *eclipses and planetary alignments that fall into a definite (or non-random) "pattern."* These types of events would form a special symmetrical pattern that is essential for recognizing them as "out of the ordinary."

The presence of a pattern implies that a pattern maker was at work and that is basically what this study is attempting to show.

It would naturally follow that the symmetrical pattern would validate its credibility in that it would sync up with the Biblical calendar and support the prophetic narrative. This makes much more sense.

I continued my studies with a DVD by Mark Biltz called *Linking Eclipses to the Coming of Messiah*. The information he discovered was important because it revealed both a visual "pattern-based" and timed "calendar-based" methodology was being used by God in presenting lunar and solar eclipse-type signs. Mark nailed it with his presentation and the floodgates were open.

Here are the key examples of total lunar eclipses (blood moons) that we have.

The three lunar tetrad sets of 1949-50, 1967-68 and 2014-15 *all* had perfectly synchronized appearances on the feast days of Passover and Tabernacles.

There is no way that this could have been an accident.

Bear in mind these two factors: First, the vantage point for observing this phenomenon is planet Earth. Second, the two named feasts are typically celebrated by "Earthlings." There is also a *chronological order* revealed by the way the pattern of feasts are arranged (per year) within each of the three tetrads.

Passover occurs *first*.

The children of Israel (in Egypt) followed the instructions of Moses, prepared the Passover, packed up, left Egypt, and finally crossed over the Red Sea.

Could this represent or mirror a prophetic future end times Exodus/Harpazo (Rapture) event?

Tabernacles occurs *second*.

This is the last of the yearly feasts where all believers are assembled together to fellowship with God. Could this represent or mirror a prophetic future gathering together of all the saints to be with Jesus Christ after his Second Advent?

Remember, the construction and use of the original tabernacle, for the purpose of fellowship with God, happened *after* the Passover/Exodus event. There is always some knowledge to be gained from anything that God does, and I believe that in this case, the specific order has a specific meaning.

My conclusion here would be that, in the unique pattern that is shown by the tetrads, there is a resulting message. What could this message be?

Answer: The Tetrads could be a prelude message notification for the following: First, an upcoming Rapture (Passover is referenced) of the church. Second, the celebration of fellowship (Feast of Tabernacles is referenced) with Jesus Christ together with *all* of His people.

Hopefully this section will give better understanding of the pattern recognition factor that is featured in the Lunar Tetrads.

For more information on the eclipse cycles that have direct correlation to the Biblical calendar, please go online and search for Mark Biltz and *Linking Eclipses to the Coming of Messiah* and/or his book entitled *Blood Moons*.

Example 4

Revelation 12 is an important section that describes widescope prophetic history (past, present, and future) that is consistent with the Biblical narrative. It also provides insight into the celestial method God uses to convey information.

Rev 12:1 says: "And there appeared a great wonder in heaven; a woman clothed with the sun, and the moon under her feet, and upon her head a crown of twelve stars..."

This section makes full use of imagery that works by means of two narratives that parallel each other. That is the methodology and the key that unlocks it.

However, the interweave of these narratives is amazing in that they tell the prophetic story by means of character association and still manage to provide details that have an accurate representation in astronomy.

A *character-based* narrative, with the figures as follows: The **Woman** is Virgin Mary / Israel; **Leo** is The Lion / Tribe of Judah; The **Dragon** is Satan.

An *astronomically-based* narrative, with the constellations as follows:

"Woman clothed with the sun and the moon by her feet" refers to Virgo with the sun (solar) located next to the shoulder and the moon (lunar) located next to the foot.

In ancient times as well as today, the clothing that women (and men) wore generally hung from the shoulders, thus the phrase "clothed with the sun" is both appropriate and accurate.

"A crown of twelve stars above her head" refers to Leo located above Virgo with the addition of Mercury, Mars, and Venus in alignment (9-23-17) so as to create a complete outline of a form that could resemble a tall head piece or "crown."

"Great red dragon" refers to Draco and contains a star called Ethanin that is located in head part of the constellation and is a red star giant that creates the red color in this formation. The definition of Ethanin in Hebrew is "the long serpent or dragon."

An important prophetic celestial link: One more time: Rev 12:1 says "And there appeared a great wonder in heaven; a woman clothed with the sun, and the moon under her feet, and upon her head a crown of twelve stars…"

- The concept of royalty here is implied, because the woman is wearing the type of headwear that someone of royal status would have on their heads.
- The woman (Virgo) is representative of the nation Israel.
- Leo is representative of a Royal line (Judah) within Israel.
- The size of the Leo 12-star crown formation is unusually large (comparatively speaking) when viewed next to Virgo. In other words, it's a really big hat.

Is there any historic data (biblical and secular) that would associate this Leo 12-star formation with an actual crown and place it within a royal Hebrew context?

Yes there is. The story in Genesis (chapters 37 - 50) of Joseph in Egypt reveals this association.

The general time frame examined here is from around 1797-1640 BC. The Torah was written by Moses sometime around 1272 BC, after the Exodus. Go back 440 years (400 years of Egyptian captivity plus 40 years wandering in the wilderness) and we arrive at 1712 BC. This is roughly the transitional period between the 14th and 15th dynasties.

As the story goes, Joseph was one of twelve children belonging to Jacob (Israel), and he was sold into slavery by his spiteful brethren. But later, through divine circumstance, he became a very powerful leader in Egypt.

In fact, the extent of authority that Pharaoh gave to Joseph was to make him second in command, second only to number one, and that person was Pharaoh himself.

Before rising to this status, Joseph endured hatred and betrayal from his brethren, suffered greatly and unjustly, and eventually overcame it all. Sound familiar?

A little side note: There are twelve sons of Israel, twelve stars mentioned in Rev 12:1 and twelve stars in the extremely rare Leo constellation crown formation of 9-23-17.

As a leader in this new position, Joseph was given all the perks that go along with that level of prestige: a new house, a new wardrobe with accessories, a new signet ring, a new chariot, etc. He would also have been given something special to wear that identified him as ruler over all of Egypt, which meant both the "upper" and "lower" provinces. That special item was a crown or the Royal proper "double crown" of Egypt.

There are many types of royal crowns throughout history, and I'm not going to try to list them all here. I think that most people would agree that a typical crown is usually a one-piece unit, anywhere from 3 to 8 inches in height and embellished with shiny baubles.

But this Egyptian crown was a unique dual headpiece

arrangement. It had one headpiece for the upper province and another headpiece for the lower province that when put together, formed the total "double" crown.

This double crown is a real piece of work. It looks like a bucket with a single prong extending upward on its backside and a cone in the center that looks like a bowling pin. Jutting out from the front-middle area of the bowling pin is a single curly-ended antenna piece.

This extension is probably representative of the cobra snake. We can all agree that a cobra snake is not to be messed with. So in my opinion, this over-the-top crown is a bold and in-your-face expression of power, authority, and reach.

The single antenna with the curl at the end does have a definite resemblance to the uppermost section of the Leo constellation. The uppermost section of Leo (neck and head) actually ends with a bit of a curl that when compared to the double-crown, makes for an astounding match.

We can also conclude that this particular double-crown is unique, in that it's shaped differently and much bigger than most typical crowns that we're familiar with. This interesting *proportional* factor is also seen in the graphic collage (at the end of this chapter) that shows the "very large crown" over the head of the "wearer" (Virgo) of the crown.

Anyway, let's get back to bridging the gap between Joseph's royal crown and a future celestial royal crown counterpart.

We can basically conclude that there's a correlation between Joseph (second under Pharaoh) and the use of the big royal double-crown of Egypt. And although it may be considered a loose connection, it's still a connection.

Further back in time, King Mentuhotep II ruled over Egypt from approximately 2061 to 2010, and there's a rock relief that shows him wearing the double crown. So the double crown was indeed standard attire for that era and beyond.

Joseph would certainly have been wearing the same type of attire, in his second-in-command leadership role over both Upper and Lower Egypt, in a subsequent dynasty. (To see more information on the use of the Egyptian double crown with photos, please visit Wikipedia and look up Mentuhotep II.)

In my opinion, which now has some historical backing, the Leo 12-star configuration and its comparative symmetry is meant to send a message. I believe that the message is announcing a visit from Royalty.

Regarding additional verifiable correlations, no one debates the fact of the Chinese records (data) in the area of astronomy as anything other than remarkably accurate. Their sophistication in this particular scientific discipline was unmatched by any other culture in its time.

Gil Broussard is a researcher who has done some incredible work in using this data to find those correlations. His idea was to do an overlay of real, documented data from the Chinese astronomical records against the timelines of the major catastrophes that are written about in the Old Testament

Guess what? It worked. The celestial events can be shown to have a direct correlation to many of the major catastrophes of the Old Testament. The cause and effect principle does apply here, and the causal factors that are in play are "celestial" in nature.

Gil Broussard, in much the same way as Rick Larson and Mark Biltz, has helped to connect the dots. Please look up Gil on the web and check out his information.

The Biblical character-based and astronomically-based signs are now exposed, and there's a clear match between the characters and their celestial counterparts.

The concept is so amazingly simple: God puts the dots out there. Connect the dots, see the characters.

Watch the characters interact, see the storyline.

Follow the storyline to its ultimate conclusion.

Hopefully, you won't casually dismiss the information presented in this book, but consider the entire body of information. See if the celestial storyboard makes any sense. After that's done, go ahead and reach your conclusion.

The bottom line is that Israel appears to be the geographic focal point with regard to Messiah. This relationship also works in conjunction with the "great wonder in heaven" sign that the Apostle John saw in Revelation 12.

But there's still more Israel-centric data that needs to be looked at.

Lunar Tetrad of 1949–50

April 13
1949
Passover

October 7
1949
Tabernacles

April 2
1950
Passover

September 26
1950
Tabernacles

Lunar Tetrad of 1967–68

April 24
1967
Passover

October 18
1967
Tabernacles

April 13
1968
Passover

October 6
1968
Tabernacles

Lunar Tetrad of 2014–15

April 15
2014
Passover

October 8
2014
Tabernacles

April 14
2015
Passover

September 28
2015
Tabernacles

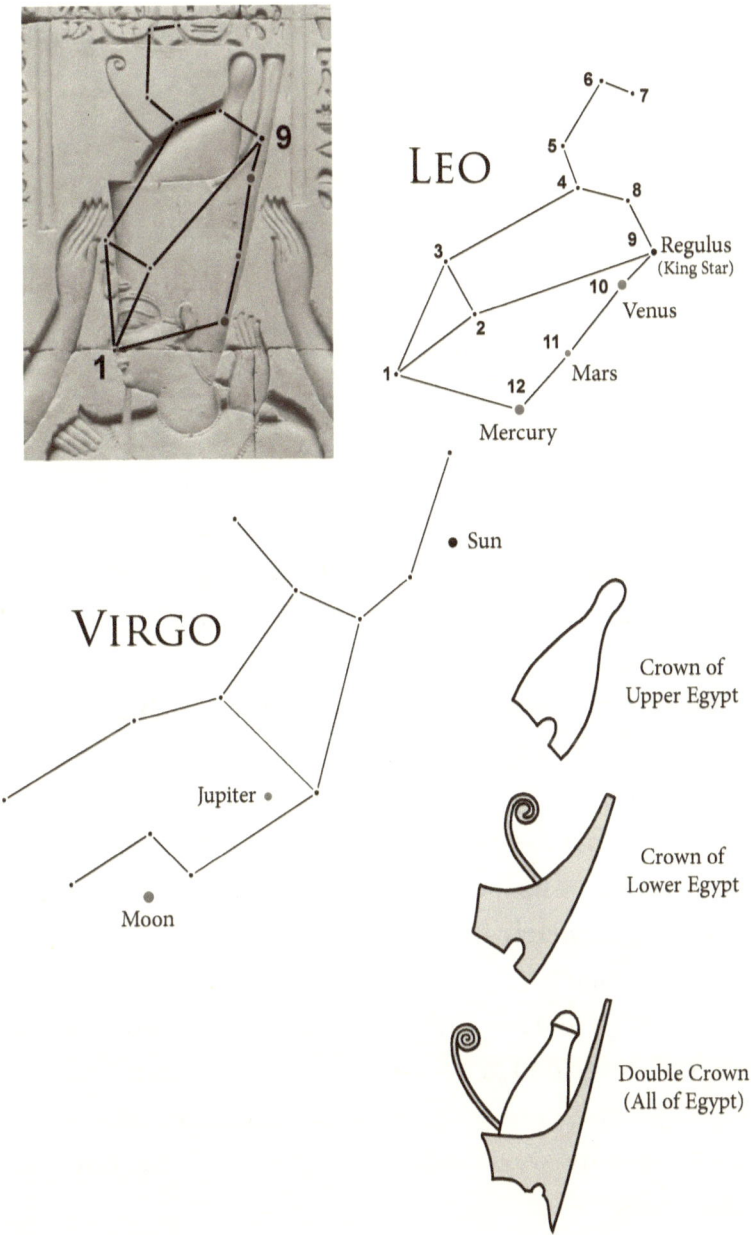

The resemblance between the Virgo–Leo astronomy of September 23, 2017 and the royal double crown of Egypt is unmistakably obvious.

6

Anyone Want A Good Used ... Calendar?

Back to Y2K. If Y2K (year 2000) had everyone on edge due to its supposedly ominous "time's up doom's here" reputation, why did it not produce anything ominous as far a literal event?

Answer: Because the year 2000 is not synchronized to the calendar system for which the ominous future event was planned.

It seems that the prophetic relevance of the Y2K threshold, in terms of its location on our current Gregorian calendar, is completely lost.

Why is that?

Answer: It started with a man in ancient Rome named Julius who decided he wanted his own "standardized" calendar system. A guy with that much arrogance and power gets to have his way. Besides, the glory of Rome knew no limitations.

The Julian calendar is solar-based, and it works based on the one year (365 days, 5 hours, 48 minutes to be exact) of time that it takes for the Earth to complete a full orbit around the sun. He got some help in devising the new system from an Alexandrian astronomer named Sosigenes.

The system that was in place prior to that, the Roman calendar, was a more complex lunar-based system utilizing moon-phase orientation that required regular adjustments. This was done to maintain synchronization with the equinox and solstice cycles. It worked for the most part, and time marched on.

Regarding leap years, the Julian system determined that one should fall every fourth year. A leap day was added in the fourth year in the month of February. However this calculation was incorrect in that it was inserting too many leaps. What this did was throw the timing of the established charted astronomical events "off sync" with the major religious holidays like Easter which follows Passover.

Passover historically syncs up with the first full moon after the vernal equinox.

Did you catch that?

Let me rephrase it in a few different ways. As a result of this calendar modification, a very important religious holiday called "Easter" (right after Passover) was offset or displaced from a significant astronomical association. The astronomical sign value of this special event was basically removed from sight. The celestial storyboard got an unwelcome paint job. Interesting, isn't it?

But Julius Caesar got his way, the former calendar was deposed, and his new calendar system was implemented.

My case against Julius works like this.

There was a lot of business that Julius had to deal with in the way of government administration, military conquest, civilian oversight, municipal infrastructure, watching his back, and on and on.

So why in the world would he take time out of his busy schedule to mess with the calendar? The sundials of every town in the empire were working just fine. Everyone knew the timing for the agricultural cycles like the backs of their hands. If it ain't broke, don't fix it.

The answer: Maybe there was someone lurking (operating) in the shadows who was influencing his thinking—or pulling his spiritual strings.

Well, hang in there folks because this slick little timeline slight-of-hand has a happy ending.

The Julian calendar had some serious problems. Over the centuries, it became apparent that the timing had drifted and was off sync. There was now a very apparent 10-day advance that marked the variation between the written calendar and the celestial clockworks.

In the late 1500s, Pope Gregory XIII decided to fix the problem. He did his calculations, developed the solution and implemented it. An adjustment to shorten the average solar year by the amount of 0.0075 days was introduced. This fix did the trick to get things properly synchronized again.

As a result, the timing of the lunar cycle that corresponds to a very important religious holiday called "Easter" was effectively brought back into line. The celestial sign value of this special sacred event was restored back to its former established timing pattern or what I call "prophetic sync." Isn't that interesting?

This timing correction then became the new standard: the Gregorian calendar. This is the same calendar system that is used worldwide today.

Did all this calendar shuffling over the centuries totally displace the original calendar system that was in use prior to Julius? Did this timing "shell-game", played by the world's elite, cause God to concede and throw in the towel?

No, it did not. But it did reorient the entire world in such a manner as to break sync with the original foundational calendar system that was instituted by God.

Good news though. The original foundational calendar system is still in use today, but it is referred to as the Hebrew calendar. Fortunately, this unique people group has retained use of this calendar from the time of their founder, Abraham.

But, as documented in Genesis chapter 6, the use of this original legacy calendar system was already in place prior to Abraham. Noah's flood has references to specific months and dates in it. This is clear evidence of an established working calendar system that pre-dates Abraham.

Apparently the pre-flood antediluvians weren't a bunch of hairy-knuckle-dragging cave dwellers after all. They had agriculture, craftsmanship, and a calendar.

This original "legacy" clock has been ticking away unaltered for a long, long time and has been maintained through the millennium—that's a fact.

When it comes to the issue of "legacy" or "authorship," some people may try to credit the original legacy calendar system to a certain ancient culture.

For example, the Amorites (in ancient Babylon) were quite advanced in their day. Research on this particular culture has shown them proficient in the disciplines of mathematics, astronomy, architecture, construction, and yes, time tracking or calendars.

But can it be proven that they "invented" the original legacy calendar? No it can't. At best, it can be said that they utilized it.

But there is a source of information, predating the Amorites and all other human cultures, that shows authorship in regards to time tracking.

Genesis 1:14: "And God said, Let there be lights in the firmament of the heaven to divide the day from the night; and let them be for signs, and for seasons [appointments]; and for **days**, and **years**." It is obvious here that the days and years speak of a calendar system.

Some people disregard this information due to the fact of who it is that's taking the credit for the concept of a calendar. That's their choice. But the "who" in this case is also taking credit for creating the celestial realm and the celestial realm is the clocking mechanism for the calendar.

And because this celestial clocking mechanism is unquestionably beyond any human capability yet still remains a technical *fact,* any debates about authorship are rendered totally pointless. Back to finding a good doomsday calendar.

So how do we attain a better understanding of where the Y2K mark should truly be located with respect to our modern age timeline?

We know that the year 2000 AD (Gregorian) is equivalent to the year 5760 on the original legacy calendar. But that's history now. Nothing happened.

The solution?

Place the Y2K mark within the framework of the original legacy calendar and start from there. Hopefully some fog can be lifted and a more accurate picture can be developed.

So let's move on.

What year, according to the original legacy calendar system, is the equivalent of the 2000-year elapsed time period that followed the BC to AD crossover point?

That would be the year 5777, which was 2017 AD on the Gregorian calendar. It's this newly corrected Y2K (5777) mark that could possibly reveal a significant event that has true important prophetic relevance.

And exactly *what* would this significant event have been? I'm very glad you asked me!

And if you call now! . . . For just three easy payments of $29.95! . . . I'll be happy to send you the answer! And if enough people send money, I might just start a mega church, host my own TV show, and buy a couple Lear jets!!

Well, that was a lot of fun but let's move on.

Did an apocalyptic, earth-shattering end-of-it-all event occur at the end of year 5777 (2017 Gregorian)?

No, it didn't.

Shouldn't there have been something so extremely geophysically cataclysmic that it would clearly qualify as a global Revelation-style Apocalypse? I thought that there might be. But it just did *not* happen.

But wait a minute!

My research did not result in the discovery of a last and final dooms-*day*. My research led me to discover a special seven-*year* time frame, which began immediately after the supposedly dreaded year of 5777.

The end of 5777 did not produce an end-of-it-all-type event. However, there is a very significant start-of-it-all event, and it's detailed in a later chapter of this book. And it won't cost you three easy payments either. It's free.

This event was not in the form of a catastrophe. It was in the form of a signal.

The signal that was given does have very serious prophetic implications because it is in perfect sync with the Biblical legacy calendar. The celestial clockworks do have important information to convey to us via a storyboard.

But I'd like to go through this study step by step so that a solid foundation built on good data can be established. Then hopefully the lights will come on.

Patience has its rewards.

7
What's Up With the Sevens?

There are a lot of places in the scriptures where the number seven pops up.

Some appearances define time-period segments. Some are describing design elements. Some relate to judgment and some are totally out of the blue.

In the modern tech-sector tool chest, we have a couple of tools known as pattern recognition and data analysis. These are very helpful for identifying and isolating interesting stuff. Let's check out some patterns and then do some analysis.

First off. In Genesis, after God created the world in six days, He rested on the seventh day, otherwise known as the "Day of Rest" or "Sabbath."

There are seven days in a week.

In Egypt, Pharaoh had a prophetic dream that had seven good-looking cows and seven bad-looking cows in it. He also had a dream with seven good-looking stalks of wheat and seven bad looking stalks of wheat. The dream really bothered Pharaoh but he couldn't get any of his mystics to interpret it. Then God, though divine circumstance, prepared Joseph to deliver the correct interpretation to Pharaoh.

The interpretation that was given predicted a seven-year period of bumper crop followed by a seven-year period of crop failure, resulting in widespread famine.

There's a seven-year-long cycle (Deuteronomy 15) that was instituted by God for His chosen people. The seventh and last year of this cycle is important enough to have its own unique name, which is called "Shemitah."

The longer-range time span cycle given by God to Israel for them to follow is defined as seven sets of seven years totaling forty-nine years. This cycle is capped off with a fiftieth year, called a Jubilee. This Jubilee cycle serves as a reoccurring time span that is key in understanding the historical passage of time within a biblical context.

God instructed Moses to build a candle stand (menorah) with a main shaft and six additional side-extending branches (three per side) for holding a total of seven candles. Joshua had his army march around Jericho seven times. Leading the army were seven priests with seven ram's horns.

There's the story (2 Kings 4:35) about how Elisha prayed for the dead son of a Shunemite woman and watched God restore this boy back to life. After he miraculously revived, he sneezed seven times. This particular example is the one that stood out in my mind as the most astounding.

The miracle of the boy coming back to life would have

been the most absolutely stunning event ever witnessed by those around. But in all the excitement of this spectacular event, who would have ever thought to count the number of times that the boy sneezed?!

But someone (Elisha) did indeed count and then record the information. To me, this story has very special meaning in that the number seven is used in such an odd way. It's sending a message of some kind. But what is the message? I'm not sure but I can tell you this . . . it's nothing to sneeze at.

Then there's the story (2 Kings 5:14) about when Naaman, who had leprosy, visited Elisha in order to be healed of his condition. Elijah told him to go dunk himself in the Jordan River seven times. He walked up to the bank of the Jordan River, waded in, and then dunked himself seven times, and was completely healed.

In the Book of Daniel (chapter 3), the account of King Nebuchadnezzar throwing three of Daniel's friends into a furnace is given. The reason for this harsh judgment is because there was a politically motivated group within the king's administration that did not like Daniel and his friends. So they schemed to eradicate those who they considered to be their opposition.

The three friends (Shadrach, Meshach, and Abednego) who were the targets of this scheme were brought before the king, interrogated, and convicted right on the spot. Their negative response to the king's questions made him so mad that he commanded an extreme form of punishment: death by fire in a furnace. The king told the workers who maintained the furnace to increase the temperature to seven times that of its normal operating temperature.

In Daniel chapter 4, there's a bizarre account of the proud and mighty king Nebuchadnezzar being brought down to earth by a very unusual judgment issued by God. The king's heart (or mind) was changed into that of a wild beast that typically lives outdoors and eats the plants that grow on the land. The length of his punishment (Dan 4:16) was "seven times" or seven years.

Daniel's seventieth week is made up of seven years.

In the Book of Revelation, the use of the number seven increases dramatically.

In Revelation 1:4 there are seven churches mentioned.

In Revelation 1:12 there are seven golden candlesticks.

In Revelation 1:16 Christ is holding seven stars in his right hand.

In Revelation 5:1 there is a book with seven seals.

In Revelation 8:2 there's seven angels with seven trumpets.

In Revelation 15:7 there are seven angels who have seven last plagues.

In recent times, Jonathan Kahn made the discovery (Mystery of the Shemitah) that the seven-year Shemitah cycle corresponds exactly with financial disasters that plagued America—as far back as the Great Depression and right up to the latest downturn in 2014—perfectly. His discovery was so significant that certain "investor" type individuals from Wall Street contacted him to discuss it.

The seven-year Shemitah cycles have also been shown to exactly correlate with major world government power shifts, wars and other major world events in our twentieth and twenty-first centuries. The seven-year Shemitah (and Jubilee) cycles are apparently still in effect as of the writing of this book in 2019!

In 2015 there were a couple of cows (on different farms in different locations) born with the number seven on their foreheads. It was widely covered on the news and media. The number seven was formed from a patch of white fur, which was surrounded by the naturally darker contrasting colored fur. There was such a distinct sharp uniform edge in the formation of the numbers that they could not be mistaken as anything else but the number seven.

According to Biblical interpretation that assigns divine attributes to certain numbers, the number seven represents completion. The number three represents perfection. I'm not waving the flag for numerology here, but any year that happens to end with 777 (5777 = 2017 Gregorian) might be something to keep your eye on.

Could this triple play of the number seven be telling us that the year of 5777 is extremely significant?

I read the Bible from cover to cover and as I step through the pages, I inevitably will trip over the number seven.

This list of events with a seven in them is more than sufficient to establish the fact of an evident repeating pattern.

I'm sure that there are even more examples to be found that I haven't covered in this chapter.

This special number has found its way into so many varying scenarios that it almost seems to be tapping me on the shoulder. I came to the conclusion that the repetition of the number seven in Holy Scripture is meant to grab my attention.

But *why* would that be? Could it be that God wants us to *recognize* the number *seven* as a significant prophetic *indicator*?

It's well known by biblical scholars that the number seven, in terms of a divine or mystical context, means "completion." So I decided to take the hint and pay careful attention to the number seven.

In my opinion, the reoccurrence of the number seven in all these different scriptures is sending a strong message from God that we're moving towards or "ramping up" to an eventuality that features the number seven.

8

No Man Knows The Day Or The Hour

In Matthew 24:36, Jesus said regarding his Second Advent, "but of that day and hour knoweth no man." In Matthew 24:42 Jesus said regarding his Second Advent, "watch therefore for ye know not what hour your lord doth come."

Both verses actually go hand-in-hand and it's simply to make a point: even though we don't know the exact time of His return/arrival, we need to watch for it because He doesn't want us to be surprised. He wants us to be ready. The sense of the command in this text is that we are to watch and watch diligently.

It seems like when the study of end-times prophesy is discussed within church circles and the Second Advent is brought to the forefront, there's inevitably some automatic, resisting "kick-back" from someone who takes exception to it.

I'm always surprised when this happens, but I really should not be. Maybe a tad annoyed but no more than that. The person will always use this most often repeated phrase in order to curtail the subject, the ever-popular "you can't know the day or the hour."

OK, it's true that no human can know for 100% sure the day or the hour of the Second Advent, when Jesus himself returns and plants his feet on the Mount of Olives on good ol' planet Earth. Besides, when it's day on one side of the planet, it's night on the other side. So from a geographic perspective, it's impossible to know for sure.

And I'll readily admit that venturing an insightful guess is still not the same as actually "knowing." Only God **knows** and I acknowledge that fact.

But what's with the same old line being regurgitated over and over again in order to dismiss the subject?

Is it normal to express such an aversion to this often referred to and important imminent Biblical event? Is it a subject that's so dangerously taboo for most religious institutions that they need to sweep it under the rug?

I'd really like to know *something*. I mean, I'm just a naturally curious type of person. Is that really so bad? Isn't curiosity a God-given human attribute? Is there some justification for my wanting new knowledge and seeking some answers about this controversial Biblical topic?

Yes there is. The disciples wanted new knowledge. In Matthew 24:3: "Tell us, when shall these things be? and what shall be the sign of thy coming, and of the end of the world?"

In Daniel 12:4 it says "..to the time of the end: many shall run to and fro, and knowledge shall be increased." The "increase" mentioned here is not to be considered as brand new sacred revelation or prophesy. It's rather to be considered as the gaining of a *better understanding* of that which has already been written about in prophecy. It also probably includes an increase in knowledge in areas such as science.

The disciples wanted to know more. Daniel wanted to know more. Many people of this current twenty-first century generation want to know more.

The "watch therefore" words in Mat 24:42 make me think seriously about what is approaching in the near future. But the attitude of the typical modern day church individual will simply not address the "watch therefore" imperative. It's ignored for some reason. Maybe their future is totally secure. They're at ease.

But when some exciting new information that sheds light on "what to watch for" in the area of prophesy becomes available, you would think that more people of faith would be eager to check it out. And with everything that's happening in the world lately, watching current events that seem to directly correlate to prophetic texts is becoming easier and easier. These are amazing and exciting times.

The astronomy mentioned in Chapter 5 is something that should definitely prompt any Christian to stand up and pay attention. It was definitely something to watch in the days of the Wise Men, so why shouldn't it be the same today?

As bleak as this situation appears, there are still some

wise men around who are seeking for truth. These are modern day pioneers who recognize that we've got a serious twenty-first century knowledge gap and are working to fill it.

One of these Christian pioneers is a guy named L.A. Marzulli. He's a researcher who has done incredible work in the area of pre-flood civilizations, ancient technology and the paranormal. He covers these subjects in a "dig deep" manner that tackles the really tough questions that most people won't get anywhere near. Whether it's good, bad, or ugly, L.A. will research it, document it, and bring the information out into the open. He's the high beam on a dark road.

I'm going to look at just a bit of information that he's covered and extract a piece of knowledge that has a very unusual tie-in to the astronomy factor of this book. The ancient structures known as pyramids are going to be my focal point.

Throughout the world, pyramids are found. In South America especially, there are some well-preserved sites featuring these remarkable structures that tourists regularly visit.

But Egypt has the most famous site of all and that would be the Giza plateau, the home of the great pyramid of Giza.

Over the years, some of the mysteries of this monster structure have slowly been revealed. Other mysteries are unsolved and not giving up their secrets.

The matter of the sheer girth of this thing has always been a problem. It also has a complex set of deep interior chambers that are inter-connected via tunnels or shafts.

The King's chamber has a ceiling that is constructed from huge blocks of solid granite that are the size of a railroad car! This granite was apparently quarried in Aswan, which is 500 miles away.

The tools of that period were made of copper and it's simply impossible to chisel and shape granite with a softer material like copper. The placement of these megalithic granite blocks cannot be explained with the methods and manpower that were common in that day.

There's another mystery in this pyramid. There are interior shafts cut into it for some unknown purpose. Were these shafts for airflow? Were they portals for the passage of spiritual entities? Were they for the transfer of some materials between the chambers? Perhaps they were for venting of vaporous fumes or the intake of a liquid of some type? Did the pyramid run on "regular" or "diesel"?

It turns out that these angular shafts have an interesting feature that is also found in the architecture of other similar ancient pyramidal structures around the world. They have in their angular orientation a definite directional correlation to significant *astronomical events.*

The most common alignments are with the summer and winter solstices but as you'll see shortly, there are other celestial factors in play.

Nowadays, these types of alignments would be considered totally absurd. The calculations involved are simply not relevant to modern day civilization. The angular shafts are impractical and anomalous. More importantly, they don't adhere to local or national building codes!

L.A. Marzulli posed these questions and I totally agree with his line of thought.

How in the world does a thing that huge get built? Who could run a project of that scale? How can that much material be cut, moved, stacked and aligned? Where does the guy running the show get the know-how to give this monster structure a mechanism that incorporates a precise celestial bearing?

I gave this some thought because I too, like to build a project now and then. I could imagine developing, let's say, a sixty-acre site for commercial use and bringing in a GC (general contractor) to scope it out.

I'll play the "developer" in this scene.

Developer: "Good morning GC. Thanks for stopping by the site."

GC: "Good morning."

Developer: "I've got sixty acres leveled, services are in and all the permits pulled."

GC: "Great."

Developer: "I've got two types of structures in mind. I want you to pick the one you'd like to build."

GC: "OK. What are my choices?"

Developer: "One is a pyramid shaped structure using

one million three-foot by three-foot by four-foot solid stone blocks. The other one is a rectangular structure using concrete and steel."

GC: "Are the blocks being shipped to the site pre-cut?"

Developer: "Nope. They'll be cut here on site out of rough stock. One other thing. You'll need to cut in a straight open shaft in the deep interior of the pyramid and continue building around it so as to totally encase it with the surrounding blocks. Also, the shaft needs to be set to a precise angle of 26.3 degrees that will provide for the perfect alignment with a star called Regulus (the King star) on the exact day of Rosh Hashanah (Hebrew New Year) on September 20, 2017."

GC: "You mean the star called Regulus that's a part of the constellation called Leo which is located above Virgo?" (Note: My GC just happens to know about astronomy. ☺)

Developer: "Yes. That Regulus. What do you think?"

GC: "This is a no-brainer. I'll build the rectangle."

Well, I hope you enjoyed the trip to my little construction site. But here's the deal. The Pyramid at Giza has some knowledge incorporated into it that seems to point to a design that's based on a divine blueprint.

There actually was the occurrence of this exact same astronomical event in the Pyramid of Giza. And it has a tie-in to the information that I want to relay to you. Inside the great pyramid of Giza there's actually one of its interior shafts set to an ascending angle that is configured to precisely 26.3 degrees.

And on Rosh Hashanah (New Year) Sep 20 of 2017 (5777), the star that was directly in alignment with this particular interior shaft was Regulus in the constellation of Leo. It just so happened that Venus (the Morning star) also fell into perfect alignment at this exact same time.

Was that just a coincidence or fluke? I don't think so.

This alignment is obviously oriented in such a manner as to bring into question the construction plans for the Giza pyramid. This particular celestial orientation is clearly indicating a tie-in to the constellation of Leo and the timing is clearly indicating a "closing out" of the year 5777. The structural mechanism cleverly incorporates two important aspects of the **celestial** (visual = storyboard) and the **timing** (calendar = schedule) to say something that is prophetically significant.

So my question is this . . . *who drew up the building plans?*

Answer: I don't know for sure but I'm going to venture a guess: it's the exact same person who encoded so many of the world's major events into the Torah.

At this point, I have to mention a person who has also researched this area and has amassed a wealth of incredible information on it. Daniel Matson has many articles at *watchfortheday.com* and you definitely should check them out. The mathematics he's discovered that correlate the astronomy will astound you.

It's precisely this type of outside-the-box knowledge increase that gives a sense of awe when you realize that it's all just too perfect not to have been planned.

Does this new knowledge (data) reveal the day or the hour? No it does not. But is it possible that this data reveals a pattern? I believe it does.

The question now becomes: does this pattern lead somewhere? Well, you don't have to send me three easy payments of $29.95. But you do have to be open minded and read on.

First I want to have some more fun with my sixty-acre building site.

Developer: "By the way, I need the driveway and parking lot done."

GC: "I can take care of that."

Developer: "Great. Do you see those pallets over there?"

GC: "Yup."

Developer: "That's forty pallets of standard base material, thirty pallets of volcanic ash mix, twenty pallets of lime mix, and ten pallets of sea salt."

GC: "What's that for?"

Developer: "It's for a special ancient Roman concrete formula that I want used."

GC: "Really? What's the mix?"

Developer: "It's the standard base material with the addition of the volcanic ash, lime and salt water. That's what will be mixed and poured right here onsite. It will cure to a PSI (pounds per square inch) that's much higher than regular Portland and it will last thousands of years."

GC: "But if you do that we won't have to come back in ten years to redo your driveway and parking lot!" ☹

Pause for a moment of silent contemplation.

Well reader, has your knowledge about concrete increased?

Back to the modern day church culture for a moment. The new knowledge that is sought by the few is apparently deemed to be irrelevant by most. That's a bummer. The negative response is generally expressed in two ways:

- We find the new information is somewhat interesting, but it's not an essential part of the gospel so it's not worth the effort to study.

- We find new information of this type to be far too radical and we don't want that kind of stuff making waves in our congregation.

They don't seem to be interested in "knowing" about any new scientific information that could give valuable insight to end-times prophesy. They don't seem to be interested in "knowing" about the geopolitical activities occurring on the national and international scene that affect our lives. They don't seem to be interested in "knowing" about the extent of massive geo-physical catastrophes that are happening worldwide and that they clearly relate to what's written in Matthew 24.

So what then, *do* they know?

They know this—"You can't know the day or the hour"—and that's about all. The really sad thing about this is that their teachers routinely use the same line.

This kind of disregard or skepticism is much more that a random or sporadic situation within church society. It's absolutely rampant.

Looks like we have a conundrum here that needs to be solved. Here's a possible solution.

There's a way to properly interpret this ever-popular, clichéd method of disregarding the quest for an increase of prophetic end-times knowledge.

This common method of disregard is not a seemingly innocent ignorance (ignorance is bliss), and it's not hard-line skepticism. It's actually born of the Laodicean spirit. That's right . . . the **Laodicean** spirit.

Any true believer would naturally seek for truth and this certainly applies to the "watching" aspect of Mat 24:42. There would be a sincere desire to know more.

Because this book seeks in part to locate current church civilization within a proposed prophetic timeline framework, and if that proposed timeline framework is indeed as close to the Second Advent as indicated, then this present day church culture would obviously be the one to immediately precede the Second Advent.

That would mean that this present day church culture *is* the Laodicean church or the latter stages of it (see Rev 3:20-22).

The thing is this. Maybe you're reading this book and the little warning lights on your dashboard are starting to come on. Maybe your interest is being brought out of a state of slumber. Maybe you're beginning to recognize some of this information (new knowledge) as potentially valuable data.

If that's happening, then don't be so easily swayed by the "you can't know" folks.

But by all means continue to study, and be sure to watch.

Over the last ten years or more, I've heard many experts in the area of prophesy voice their concerns about the convergence of end-times signs that are appearing all over the world and in the sky. Their quest for new knowledge has been successful and they're doing what they can to spread the news.

At the same time they're expressing frustration and amazement that most of the church doesn't seem to care. The mood is one of exasperation.

I'd like to tell them that they can now stop being frustrated and confused by the conundrum. This situation, in my opinion, is definitely not a fluke. It's actually a very precise indicator of where we are in history: the tail end of the Laodicean church era.

This trend is something that indirectly served as a marker in the creation of the timeline chart in this book.

The type of end-time knowledge increase that Gabriel spoke of has been in progress and is rapidly accelerating. It includes new data from both the terrestrial and celestial realm. Also, when Gabriel said that knowledge in the end-times would increase, he didn't say that the increase would go on for a while and then stop. The increase was to be ongoing or continual.

So let's continue.

9

Daniel's Prophesy of the Seventy Weeks

The Book of Daniel, chapter 9:20-27 and chapter 12:1-13, gives very important prophecies that pertain to Israel and Messiah.

The Daniel 9 prophecies provide a broad scope view on Messiah in his First Advent, the rejection of his Kingship and the end-time in which he returns at his Second Advent. This broad seventy-week (or 490 year) time span description provides a rough outline of the major events that mark these areas of prophesy.

The "end-time" reference is believed by many to be the same time that our current population is living in right now, the twenty-first century.

The Daniel 12 prophecies specifically focus on the Great Tribulation (three and a half years or 1,260 days) and the two post-tribulation time segments that are situated at 1,290 and 1,335 days. The Great Tribulation ends at the Second Advent.

This chapter seeks to explain the prophecies of Daniel, the time-line definitions and the correlations to the Book of Revelation. It also presents correlations to our present modern age.

Explaining Daniel's background in Babylon

Before Daniel became a major figure in this story, the prophet Jeremiah warned Israel to change their ways or they would invite the wrath of God.

Israel would have none of that. So the protective barrier that God had placed around Israel was lifted. The Babylonian army came into their country, overtook it, and took many people away as captives, while leaving some to remain, albeit in a servitude role.

Daniel was part of the captive group taken to Babylon. He and some of his friends were screened for certain qualities that the hierarchy deemed valuable.

Fortunately they passed the test. With this good standing, they were able to survive and thrive under their new management.

After some time, how long I'm not sure, he read the writings of Jeremiah and gained some understanding of the reason for their situation. It wasn't merely a random military conquest of one nation by another. It was a matter of God's people not following His instructions, disregarding His Holiness and finally provoking His wrath. This concept is a total mystery to many people.

But to those who know that pushing your luck too far may have divine consequences, the concept is very real.

Daniel eventually understood (Dan 9:2) what Jeremiah's prophecy was and came to terms with it. He also found some hope in the prophecy. There was a time limit to their captivity. God had actually foretold the exact duration of Israel's punishment. There would someday be a return.

Gabriel explains the seventy weeks to Daniel

Daniel, expressing deep remorse over their situation, still looked ahead to better times. He kept his faith. That must have been what sustained him.

This section begins in Daniel 9, when Daniel was praying in earnest.

Dan 9:21: "Yea, whiles I was speaking in prayer, even the man Gabriel, whom I had seen in the vision at the beginning, being caused to fly swiftly, touched me about the time of the evening oblation."

Daniel wasn't even finished his prayer when the archangel Gabriel came to visit him and relay some important end-time information directly from God.

As it was with Daniel, so it is with many of us: he wanted to know the future.

What is it that lies up ahead? That always seems to be the nagging question. In this case, the "up ahead" was actually way up ahead and practically out of sight!

The extra up ahead, which spoke of the end-times and the Second Advent, was probably too much for him to handle in one single discourse. And the gaps in the information pertaining to the end-times led Daniel to frustration.

Gabriel explains in Daniel 9:23: "At the beginning of

thy supplications the commandment came forth, and I am come to shew thee; for thou are greatly beloved: therefore understand the matter, and consider the vision." Gabriel then gave Daniel the answers to his questions and even some vital bonus material. Here's how it works and some of the actual historical details that were involved.

Daniel 9:24-27 gives three time span segments totaling seventy weeks (490 years) that are broken into three parts of seven weeks, sixty-two weeks and one week. One week equals 7 years.

The first (seven-week) time segment began with the official order (commandment to restore) by Artaxerxes for the rebuilding of Jerusalem (Neh 2:1-8). This period would also see the appearance of "Messiah the Prince."

The second (sixty-two-week) time segment (Messiah cut off) led up to the crucifixion of Jesus Christ.

The last (one-week or seventieth week) time segment simply did not happen back then.

Some people think that the events of 70 AD in Jerusalem make the case for the "antichrist" scenario, but that was only a part of a much larger picture. It was actually a foreshadowing example that can be analyzed for the purposes of gaining understanding about when the future real deal antichrist comes on the scene. God, in some instances, provides these mirror image "types" for us to study and become knowledgeable about the future reality.

The first century history of Jerusalem does have an antichrist type representation in the person of Antiochus

Ephiphanes. He was the Roman ruler who destroyed Jerusalem in 70 AD and also defiled their temple. But he was not the literal antichrist of the end-times.

And though the temple was indeed defiled in 70 AD in an abominable act, and the place was desolated, the fact remains: the other prophetic events in verse 24 did not happen. The everlasting righteousness was not brought in, the vision and prophecy was not sealed up and the most "Holy" (capital H = Christ) was not anointed. Also, if we consider from the Book of Revelation how the real antichrist will control global finance, nobody back in 70 AD took a "mark of the beast."

These specific events are characteristically end times-type events that have definite correlations in the Book of Revelation. This means that the appearance and conclusion of the seventieth week is still pending.

Included in all this news from Gabriel was the added bonus of the eventual appearance of the promised Messiah. This is what made the prophecy special above all other previous sacred texts. It was this news that finally gave credence to the name of Emanuel or, "God with us." It was very welcome information even though it would happen after Daniel's time on Earth had expired.

But even though Daniel knew that this was going to be too far out in the future to enjoy experiencing himself, he must have been very enthusiastic about it. After all, this was not just a visitation of Messiah, but the living God, the Creator. And He was coming to Daniel's hometown! That's serious stuff. Wouldn't you be a bit anxious after hearing something like that? We'll see a bit of Daniel's angst a little later in this chapter and get a sense of the anticipation that he felt.

Moving now to Daniel 9:27 from the Greek Septuagint manuscript: "And one week shall establish the covenant with many: and in the midst of the week my sacrifice and drink-offering shall be taken away: and on the temple [shall be] the abomination of desolations; and at the end of time an end shall be put to the desolation."

The last part of verse 27 says "and at the **end of time** an end shall be put to the desolation." This means that the *total* fulfillment and conclusion of all the events in verse 27 happens at a future "end time" or more precisely at the end of the Great Tribulation.

This future seventieth week (seven-year time span) has often been referred to as the Tribulation period or Great Tribulation. Further ahead in this chapter, I show this to be incorrect. The Tribulation (i.e. Great Tribulation) is actually a three-and-a-half-year period that fits into the latter half of Daniel's seventieth week time frame.

According to Zechariah 14:9, this period also finally concludes human governorship over the world and ushers in the literal physical return of Jesus Christ to take over as King of planet Earth and establish His eternal kingdom.

The Book of Daniel is known for the famous "handwriting on the wall" account in Dan 5:5-30 where King Belshazzar was the guy who rejected the concept of divine consequences. He paid the price for it.

There's a story in Dan 6 where some of the king's officials (accusers) set Daniel up and forced him into a den of lions. The plot failed, Daniel was *taken up* from the lion's den with no harm done. His accusers were then *cast in* and suffered the *wrath* of the lions. They rejected the concept of divine consequences and paid the price for it.

The thematic thread that runs continuously through the Book of Daniel is clearly meant to warn of divine consequences that occur at the end of the line.

Daniel's seventieth week is understood to be the prophetic "end of the line." Might Daniel's seventieth week make a calendar appearance in our age?

The math and the breakdown

Recap of the math method for the "weeks": 1 week = 7 years. Daniel's prophesy has seventy weeks total, divided into three segments of 7, 62 and 1, which equates to a sum total of 490 years:

> 7 weeks = 49 years → fulfilled
> (command for the rebuilding of Jerusalem issued by Artaxerxes in 450 BC / Neh 2:1-8)
>
> 62 weeks = 434 years → fulfilled
> (crucifixion of Jesus Christ in 33 AD)[1]

---

[1] For more information on this date of 33 AD, please watch the *Star of Bethlehem* DVD by Rick Larson and see the section "Dating Christ's Execution."

1 week = 7 years → not yet fulfilled
(Conclusion of the church age and the return of Christ Messiah)

Total completed thus far = 483 years (69 weeks)
Total uncompleted = 7 years (the seventieth week)

Daniel's seventieth week is due to get plugged into world history sooner or later and many of "this generation" (Mat 24:34) are thinking: *where is it?*

Finding a good location for the seventieth week is going to require strict guidelines. It needs to follow prophetic Biblical principles, and any relevant astronomical indicators should also have a basis in scripture. It either works right or it doesn't work at all.

And who knows, maybe situated within that placement is a sub-component caught up/Rapture event and a Time of Jacob's Trouble or Great Tribulation.

The time of the end will bring an increase in "knowledge"

Dan 12:4, Gabriel to Daniel: "But thou O Daniel shut up the words and seal the book to the time of the end: **many shall run to and fro** and **knowledge shall be increased**."

Daniel was making good progress in accumulating new knowledge. From a starting point at Dan 9:21, the new information that Gabriel imparted continued all the way up to Dan 12:3. Daniel did manage to take it all in. It's quite a lot of future history to record, but he managed to get the job done. I think that he would have studied this material many times after it was initially taken down.

What I find really interesting is that even after all this intake of new knowledge, Daniel still wanted to learn more. But Gabriel cut him off: "shut up the words . . ." That's enough future for now. Take a break.

I believe that we are in that future now. If there ever was a time where it could be said that travel and knowledge has increased, it's right now in the twenty-first century. The last hundred years have produced advancements that are unparalleled in history.

Modern travel (running to and fro) comes in many forms: on land, on the sea, and even through space. Whether local, national or international, it's fast and easy.

Knowledge has really increased within the last ten years via digital tech. Even more so lately as we use our advanced technology for R&D in order to push the tech envelope even further. The computer is the tool that makes that possible.

What is also very important to *know* about what makes the days in which we live so relative and identifiable with Dan 12:4, and what makes us unlike any previous culture, is this. Our present culture regularly makes use of devices that have "knowledge" pre-installed (imprinted) into them at the manufacturing stage. These are more commonly known as operating systems (OS), software programs and applications (apps).

What's also unique about this technology (chip sets) is that it has permeated almost every single type of machine, device, and gadget known to man. This essentially has created an electronic "dependency" which is irrevocable.

Well, so far the venerable toothbrush is safe, but who knows what's next?

Artificial intelligence (AI) is already being deployed worldwide. It's the next level of tech that evidences the fact of Daniels prophetic knowledge increase. It does unfortunately have a serious downside too. The "functional" artificial intelligence tech still necessitates an input of software code. And the nature of that code depends on the intentions of the person who's writing it, doesn't it?

To get some perspective on how the acceleration of the increase in knowledge applies to our day and age, let's go back a bit. Back a hundred to a hundred and fifty years or so. Things were different. The air was fresher. The water was cleaner. The soil wasn't depleted. The cows didn't have electronic tags attached to their ears.

Life back then was built around the things that were necessary for survival. Things like farming, feeding the animals, gathering eggs into the basket, milking the cow, churning the butter, canning the fruit, walking out to the well to fill the water buckets and bringing them back to the house, chopping the firewood, fixing the plow, hitching the horse to the wagon, riding the wagon into town, visiting the general store, making a deal to sell your grain harvest to the mill, riding the wagon back to the farm, filling the water troughs, cleaning out the cattle stalls and chicken coops, mending the fence, grooming the horse and putting him back in the barn, off to church on Sunday and back to work on Monday.

Sound like fun? Things have sure changed (progressed) haven't they?

I'm not trying to spoil the party here, but the verse in Dan 12:4 also identifies this particular time, presumably the time that is *now*, as the time of the end.

In my opinion, the increase in knowledge that Gabriel spoke of is not exclusive to modern day technology. There must be a spiritual aspect involved too. The increase of knowledge in Holy Scripture and especially prophecy is what I'm referring to.

Back to Dan 12:4: "But thou O Daniel shut up the words and seal the book to the time of the end: many shall run to and fro and knowledge shall be increased."

Given that God is informing mankind of a "time of the end", it would stand to reason that he is genuinely concerned for mankind. He sent Christ Messiah to the planet Earth for this very reason.

After Gabriel told Daniel to stop writing and shut up the words, he might have thought that was the end of the story. But new information kept coming from Gabriel. The data kept flowing.

The reason? God knew that Daniel was actually desperate for more knowledge, a final conclusion. He knew that

Daniel wanted to get a look at the person from verse 9:27 who would establish the covenant and finally put an end to the desolation.

Dan 12:5: "Then I Daniel looked, and, behold, there stood other two . . ."

Dan 12:6: "And one said to the **man clothed in linen, which was upon the waters of the river** . . ."

He understood that the person who was upon the waters was Christ Messiah.

Dan 12:7: "And I heard the man clothed in linen, which was upon the waters of the river, when he held up his right hand and his left hand unto heaven, and sware by him that liveth for that it shall be for a **time, times, and a half**; and when he shall have accomplished to scatter the power of the holy people, all these things shall be finished.

Wait a minute. He was supposed to say *"seven times"*!

Seven times equals seven years! The seventieth week is seven years long! Time, times and a half only equals three and a half years! There must be some mistake!

So Daniel kept raising the question.

Dan 12:8: "What shall be the end of these things?"

Daniel had the blueprint for the seventy weeks from back in Chapter 9. He had a good understanding of the timing and details of the future events that comprised the seven-week segment and the forty-nine-week segment. Those were a done deal. He understood the man wearing linen and standing on the water was Christ Messiah.

He understood that Christ Messiah would be the one to

finish all things.

Daniel's question could be rephrased in this way: "This is all great, but where exactly is the *seventieth week?*"

This is the same question that I have and many others have. That's why we're watching the end-times signs so closely. We want to increase our knowledge in the hope of finding it.

The three-and-a-half-year time factor that links Daniel to Revelation

The Great Tribulation = 3½ years, not 7 years. There is a key time-span reference in Daniel 8:25 and 12:7 that corresponds exactly to a time-span reference that is found in the Book of Revelation.

The reference is to the duration of the last half of Daniel's seventieth week as "time, times and a half" which helps to identify this section as the same as in Rev 12:14.

This data could be essential for helping to locate Daniel's seventieth future week within our present age.

Daniel 8:23-27and 12:20-27 details the end time period that includes the final 3½-year time of trouble (i.e. "Jacobs's trouble" or the "Great Tribulation").

These verses have obvious parallels to Revelation 11 and 12 where the *exact* same three-and-a-half-year time period is described.

> Daniel 8:25, "time, times and the dividing of times".
> Daniel 12:7, "time, times and an half".
> Rev 11:2, "forty two months".

Rev 11:3, "thousand two hundred threescore days".
Rev 12:6, "thousand two hundred threescore days".
Rev 12:14, "time, times and an half".

So with a consistent end-time description in both the Book of Daniel and the Book of Revelation for the three-and-a-half-year time frame, the conclusion would have to be this: The three-and-a-half-year period in Daniel is *equal to* and the *very same* as the three-and-a-half-year period described in the Book of Revelation.

The Great Tribulation is exactly three-and-a-half-years in length. But there is an additional 75 days that occur after the three-and-a-half-year Great Tribulation, which is also included in Daniel's, prophecy.

Dan 12:11 (1,290 days) progresses forward to Dan 12:12 which states 1,335 days. 1,335 days minus 1,260 days (3½ years) equals 75 total days.

Daniel 12:12 says "Blessed is he that waiteth, and cometh to the thousand three hundred and five and thirty days.

The 1335 day count of Dan 12:12 is a further corroboration of the three-and-a-half-year Great Tribulation time frame (1,260 day count) because it's referring to people who have survived the Great Tribulation and are still alive.

Consider this: The very last event of the three-and-a-half-year (1,260 day) Great Tribulation is the War of Armageddon. Most of the planet is a disaster zone and resources are very scarce. With the exception of certain groups of people that exist in the more remote secluded areas of the planet, or underground somewhere, the remaining population is basically composed of two groups: the persecutors and the persecuted.

What kind of activity could be taking place after Armageddon is concluded that would account for a time span of 75 days?

Would these activities be similar to the ones that have happened in our own recent history with the recovery efforts after the devastation of World War I and World War II? I think the following scenario answers these questions.

- Jesus Christ Messiah takes total control and dispatches His forces to search out and round up the persecutors from around the globe.

- The remaining persecuted survivors from all over the world are rescued.

- There is a special meeting He will be attending with the remnant of Israel.

- An announcement of new authority is communicated to the entire world.

- Abundant resources are provided for a sustained recovery.

- The nations (national populations) are organized, evaluated, and promptly judged (i.e.: God performing a "separation of the sheep from the goats"), and all the persecutors as well.

Considering that Jesus Christ Messiah is noted as the person in charge of these operations, it's feasible that these activities could be accomplished in 75 days. This would bring the day count up to a total of 1335 days, which would then start the "time of blessing."

Worldwide rule at all levels under Christ's authority would be set up (Refer to Rev 21).

Daniel 9:25-27: Greek Alexandrian (LLX) Septuagint is correct and the Masoretic text is incorrect

There's a very popular teaching that says in the end times, there's a person ("he") that makes a peace treaty or covenant with the nation of Israel, which marks the beginning of the seven-year Great Tribulation.

This teaching is derived from the verses of Daniel 9:25-27 in the King James Version bible. The KJV uses a version of the Book of Daniel that was derived from the Masoretic text. The Masoretic writings are revised and edited transcriptions that featured punctuation, added words, and substituted words. In other words, modifications were made.

I believe the Masoretic transcription of Daniel is incorrect. For starters, the Greek Alexandrian LLX Septuagint manuscript predates the Masoretic revised edition, and therefore should be considered as the true authoritative source. The LLX Septuagint retained the true unaltered original format.

Dan 9:25-27 from the Greek Alexandrian LLX Septuagint reads like this:

V.25: "And thou shalt know and understand, that from the going forth of the command for the answer and for the building of Jerusalem until Christ the prince [there shall be] seven weeks, and sixty-two weeks; and then [the time] shall return, and the street shall be built, and the wall, and the times shall be exhausted."

V.26: "And after the sixty-two weeks, the anointed one shall be destroyed, and there is no judgment in him: and he shall destroy the city and the sanctuary with the prince that is coming: they shall be cut off with a flood, and to the end of the war which is rapidly completed he shall appoint [the city] to desolations

V.27: "And one week shall establish the covenant with many: and in the midst of the week my sacrifice and drink offering shall be taken away: and on the temple [shall be] the abomination of desolations; and at the end of time an end shall be put to the desolation."

Point 1: You can clearly see in verse 27 that the word "he" is *not* used before the word "shall." The Septuagint does not use the word "he" anywhere in verse 27.

Point 2: Because the word "he" is *not* found anywhere in the verse, it *cannot* be said that the establishment of the "covenant with many" is attributable to a person named "he" in verse 27. Furthermore, the covenant *cannot* be attributed to the "prince that is coming" in the latter part of verse 26 because an additional subsequent "second person" identity is *not* produced.

Point 3: The true authorship of the covenant, made with

the many (Israel = the covenant people) remains assigned to the original creator of it, which is God. Additionally, the scriptures (Exodus 29) and historical records clearly show that the sacrifices and drink offering were an offering "unto the Lord." The word "my" in verse 27 is referring to God (in the first person) as the one who is receiving these offerings.

With these three points understood, it's easy to see that correctly interpreting the end-times prophecy of Daniel 9:25-27 requires the clarity and proper context of the LLX Septuagint and nothing less. With the Greek LLX Septuagint, a much more sensible and meaningful context is realized. The theme and tenure of covenant is correctly carried through to completion.

I personally believe that what Daniel was doing in verse 27 was summarizing evil's last dying gasp in Israel. The seventieth week will produce the culmination of God's covenant with Israel. However, there will be a midpoint crisis (abomination of desolation), which finally resolves when God does away with the one that "is" the abomination that desolates. The end.

What is the root cause of the misinterpretation? The subtle redirection away from GOD in Daniel 9:27 was an error introduced by the Masorite scribes (editors) when they added the word "he" and placed it in front of the word "shall."

Clever little trick isn't it?

The Masoretic edits consisted of added words, substituted words, and added punctuation marks that were *not* in the original manuscripts. That's why Daniel 9:25-27 has been open to misinterpretation.

The idea of a prophetic scenario that is solely based on the use of an erroneous "he" in verse 27 that makes a peace deal with Israel and in so doing, kicks off a seven-year tribulation, is a very bad suggestion. But it $ells quite well.

Getting this key section of prophecy right is very important. There's a lot at stake.

Also note that verse 27 begins by giving the timeframe of 1 week (or 7 years) for the establishment of the covenant with many.

Right after that, it mentions that "in the **midst of the week**" the trouble starts. The midst would obviously be referring to a three-and-a-half-year midpoint. I believe that the trouble is actually "Jacob's Trouble" or the Great Tribulation. The chronological sequence makes sense. And if that's the case, then there's a very good chance of a harpazo/Rapture event situated just prior to that.

Daniel sure put up with a lot of grief in his life. But the multitude of life lessons that God had designed for him were not in vain.

I hope that this chapter has helped to clarify this particular area of prophecy and lift some of the spiritual fog.

With the establishment of the Great Tribulation as a three-and-a-half-year period instead of the traditional and incorrect seven-year length, this accurate hard data can confidently be used in supporting the timeline chart in this book.

Daniel's seventieth week (seven-year period) also has a more accurate definition with the inclusion of a latter-half tribulation period in which the concept of divine consequences is manifested.

With the extremely high stakes involved, when it comes to considering what lies ahead on the prophetic road, accuracy matters.

10

Moses in Egypt: Sub-Timeframe Analysis

I'd like to suggest a year for when Moses was back in Egypt to announce the ten plagues and liberate his people via the exodus. This would have been the return visit that he made, long after he fled from Egypt to the land of Midian. On older maps, Midian is shown to be located in modern day NW Saudi Arabia.

The reason I wanted to do this was to corroborate the events of the Passover, Exodus and the Red Sea Crossing with data taken from the Book of Exodus and from secular history. Doing this will help to validate the accuracy of the history in the Old Testament and will also bolster the use of "timeline" based methodology for incorporating prophetic markers.

First, I'll try to establish a rough time frame and then zero into a single year.

There are many sources for historical timelines and after looking at several of them, I found their data to be inconsistent with each other. The gaps in the various date charts were much too wide. I'm not one to simply do a copy-paste of anyone's proposed timeline and then run with it just to get some stuff out there.

I'm drawing from two reliable information sources. One is secular and one sacred.

The secular source that I'll reference will be Wikipedia, which anyone can check out at *wikipedia.org*. The reason I selected this source was because it gives a very detailed history of all the Egyptian dynasties with the associated pharaohs and their children.

More recently, Egyptian Antiquities has been able to use DNA testing to establish a more accurate royal lineage record and publish this information. This new DNA database is essential for getting the history right. When the data accumulated from archeological digs is fine-tuned with DNA results, the rabbit trails are minimized.

The 18th dynasty, which ran from 1549 to 1292 BC, is the general period of interest that I'm going to look at. It's the latter part of this dynasty, from 1353 to 1292 DC, that I'm going to examine closely.

The sacred source will be Torah. The writing of the Torah by Moses has been dated back to approximately 3300 plus years or so. It's a very thorough and detailed set of five books: Genesis, Exodus, Leviticus, Numbers, and Deuteronomy.

I'm going to assume that Moses completed this collective work towards the end of his life sometime between the age of 110 and 120 years. Deuteronomy 34:7 gives Moses age as 120 years at the time of his death.

There was an awful lot of writing for him to do and the incredibly high quality of the work could not have been accomplished during a few weekends around the campfire. The Torah was a very comprehensive volume requiring a lot of time, excellent recall of his experiences, and in-depth historical knowledge.

It also hails all the way back to the original creation. So a concise pre-flood knowledge base would also have been drawn from. There surely had to be a transfer of knowledge down through the ages beginning with Adam and his original family. Recall that their offspring knew all about God, raising livestock and agriculture. The memories of these things, and much more, could be effectively retained and communicated for a long time given their extended life spans.

Here we go.

Calculator ON.

Snickers bar ready.

The completed Torah (written after Exodus) is around 3300 plus years old.

I'm guessing that the entire set of finished scrolls were signed sealed and delivered by Moses to Joshua sometime before God called him home at the age of 120 years. That's my estimation.

In Exodus 7:7 it says "And Moses was fourscore years old (80), and Aaron fourscore and three years old (83), when they spake unto Pharaoh."

So from this data, we can establish a span of 40 years

elapsed time from the Torah handoff in the wilderness, back to the time when Moses and Aaron were confronting Pharaoh face to face in Egypt.

If we take the starting figure of 3300 years and then add 40 more years (wilderness wandering of Moses with Israel) we get a total of 3340 years.

If we put in a variance cushion of plus or minus 5 years then we get a time span range of 3335 to 3345 years.

Let's use this number range and see where it lands. As of the writing of this chapter it's 2019 AD. Go backwards in time 3335 to 3345 years and we arrive at the date range of 1316 to 1326 BC. The proper chronological BC numeric arrangement typically looks like this: 1326 to 1316 BC.

This time span range of 10 years would definitely place Moses and Aaron in Egypt at the end of the 18th dynasty.

Now let's zoom in a bit closer to look for a solid clue that could confirm that same date-range for when Moses and Aaron were in Egypt causing trouble. To find this clue, I want to study the events of the last (tenth) plague.

In Exodus, it says that the tenth plague announced by Moses was to be a visitation by an angel of death that would kill the firstborn from every family in Egypt. This also included all animal life (livestock) that they had. The exceptions to this visitation were those that observed the Passover as instructed by Moses.

And as the account goes, the angel did pass through Egypt and kill the firstborn of every single household. This included the household of the royalty who were in power at that time.

Exodus 12:29 says "And it came to pass, that at midnight the Lord smote all the firstborn in the land of Egypt, from the firstborn of Pharaoh that sat on his throne . . ."

Here's something interesting that could provide a clue. The Pharaoh that is mentioned here lost his firstborn son. If Moses had recorded the name of this Pharaoh or his son then it would easy to pinpoint that time-frame within the 18th dynasty. He didn't. But there might be some informationabout his young son that will lead to a good time frame.

From the earlier calculation that we have, Moses was stationed in Egypt at the latter part of the 18th dynasty, sometime between years 1326 to 1316 BC.

A Pharaoh of interest that was in power prior to that time period was Akhenaten (formerly named Amenhotep 4). He reigned from 1351 to 1334 BC and died sometime between the years of 1334 to 1336 BC. He had children. From among his male children, there would have been an heir to share the throne and eventually assume full authority as the new Pharaoh.

So the specific clue that we're looking for is a young man in this particular Royal line that died at a young age.

Was there a young man (a son of the now deceased Akhenaten) that would have been actively enthroned (Junior Pharaoh) *and* who also died in his youth?

Yes there was. The name of this young ruler was Tutankhamun or "King Tut." According to the history of the

18th dynasty, he officially took office in 1332 BC. His reign was from 1332 to 1323 BC (11 years total).

The details of his untimely death are sketchy at best. There has never been a conclusive cause of death established even after major studies have been done.

He apparently died at about the age of 18 or 19 in the year of **1323 BC**.

This information would make for a very good match of the account given in Exodus 12:29 where the firstborn in Pharaoh's house died.

If the Moses-Torah time-stamp data is to be verified 100% accurate, we can test it again by using the backdating formula from earlier in the chapter. The date of 1323 BC (Tut's death) should appear.

Restart the calculator.

Start at 2019 AD.

Subtract 3335 to 3345 years.

End at the date range of 1326 BC to 1316 BC.

According to Wikipedia and Egyptian historical research, Tut's death was 1323 BC and it falls right within the range of 1326 to 1316 BC. With that data, we can now confidently say that Moses was in Egypt during the 18th dynasty in the year of 1323 BC.

From that same data, we can now draw another obvious conclusion. 1323 BC was the year of the 10 plagues that God brought upon Egypt.

An interesting side note about young King Tut. On the Wikipedia site, in the Tutankhamun section, in a subsection titled "Death," the very first sentence is notable because it's saying that there are no records that detail the events of the final days of Tutankhamun's life. This is unusual because the archeology to date has produced fairly good repository of record keeping as pertaining to the affairs of the ruling class in the latter dynasties.

And why would that be the case?

Possible answer: After the 10th plague ripped through Egypt, the scribes in Pharaoh's court would have been occupied with other more important things, like shaking in their boots and hoping that they weren't next in line to get whacked.

Pharaoh's own kid wasn't the only untimely death in town. *Every* family was hit. Here's the math. If there were 500,000 families in Egypt then there would have 500,000 dead bodies. *Everyone* was in full scramble mode.

Record keeping basically took a back seat to funerals. The plagues were all done and God had made his point, so Moses didn't need to hang around. He was commissioned by God to bring the children of Israel out of Egypt and ultimately home to Mount Sinai in the land of Midian.

There's something else that needs to be checked out in order to extract another piece of important data.

The account of Exodus says that Pharaoh (the one currently presiding as king) *died in the Red Sea* while chasing down Moses and the children of Israel. In other words, he did *not* die in Egypt. We need to find a Pharaoh who meets the following three criteria:

- He was the ruler over Egypt immediately after Tutankhamun died.
- He could ride a chariot and lead an army of chariots.
- He (his mummy) has *not* been found by archeologists.

Here's the Pharaoh reign-time breakdown for the latter 18th dynasty:

- **Pharaoh Akhenaten** reigned from 1351 to 1334 BC.
- **Pharaoh Smenkhkare** reigned from 1335 to 1334 BC. This is interesting because what's happening is a brief co-ruler (overlap) arrangement with Akhenaten.
- **Pharaoh Neferneferuaten** (Queen Nefertiti/wife of Akhenaten) reigned from 1334 to 1332. This is also interesting because it's a brief co-ruler (overlap) arrangement with both Smenkhkare and Akhenaten.
- **Pharaoh Tutankhamun** reigned from 1332 to 1323 BC.
- **Pharaoh Ay** reigned from 1323 to ???

The simple "reign duration" dates prior to Tutankhamun allow us to cross off the names of Akhenaten, Smenkhkare and Neferneferuaten.

The next candidate in line is Pharaoh Ay. He began his official reign on the very same year that King Tut died, 1323 BC. This fact meets criterion number one. Let's take a closer look at Ay's background.

Prior to becoming Pharaoh, Ay was a senior advisor to Akhenaten and Amenhotep 3. This would identify him as an older man. It has been speculated that he was also the advisor to Tutankhamun and the "behind-the-scenes" power broker, which would a very reasonable assumption based on his vast experience.

And he was probably sharing a co-ruler "Pharaoh" role with King Tutankhamun because his experience would have been needed for handling difficult domestic and foreign affairs. The confrontation with Moses and Aaron was a very difficult domestic affair.

His birth name "Ay-it-netjer" translates as "Ay, Father of the God." This is quite an impressive name in that it clearly signifies supreme deity. But a badge is only as good as the person wearing it and I think there could be more to this story.

Here's an interesting fact about Ay. At the time of his role as advisor to Akhenaten, he was already an established military leader in the Egyptian army.

However, he had a particular specialty skill set that directly connects him to the Exodus. This specialty was developed during the Armarna period, which fell into the latter half of the 18th dynasty.

He was the guy in charge of the entire Egyptian cavalry.

That's right, he was the premier horse and chariot warrior of his day. This was his official title: "Overseer of All the Horses of His Majesty."

Even more significantly, this title also clearly identified Ay as the highest-ranking officer in none other than the Elite Egyptian *Chariot Division*. Here's what Exodus 14:6-9 says:

V.6: "And he made ready his chariot, and took his people with him."

V.7: "And he took six hundred chosen chariots, and all the chariots of Egypt, and captains over every one of them."

V.8: "And the Lord hardened the heart of Pharaoh king of Egypt, and he pursued after the children of Israel: and the children of Israel went out with an high hand."

V.9: "But the Egyptians pursued after them, all the horses and chariots of Pharaoh, and his horsemen, and his army, and overtook them encamping by the sea, beside Pi-hahiroth, before Ball-zephon."

This fact meets criterion number two. So far, two of three qualifiers have been satisfied. But what do the archeological records show?

Ay's tomb (WV23) was discovered in 1816 in what is called the Western Valley that's an extension from off the main entrance to the Valley of the Kings. Although the sarcophagus was found broken in pieces, the actual mummified body was absent from the tomb. There's no record of an alternate tomb for his mummy.

Archeological digs subsequent to the original discovery have not located this particular Pharaoh's mummy either. So, at the time of the writing of this chapter in June of 2019, Pharaoh Ay's mummy has still *not been found.* This fact meets criterion number three; all three criteria have now been met.

- Was Pharaoh Ay the ruler over Egypt immediately after Tutankhamun died? **YES**
- Could Pharaoh Ay ride a chariot and lead or command an army of chariots? **YES**
- Has Pharaoh Ay's mummy been found by archeologists? **NO**

With this information confirmed as true, I believe that Pharaoh Ay is the very same Pharaoh that is mentioned in the Book of Exodus as the Pharaoh who was confronted by Moses, led the chariot chase and died in the Red Sea.

Now let's take a look at the post Exodus Egyptian political situation. I want to see if there's some information that would evidence a country (Egypt) with a broken leadership in turmoil and a possible power play initiated by someone powerful who was outside the Royal line.

My theory on the post plague Egyptian political environment goes like this: If there were actually a series of supernatural catastrophes that devastated this nation and eliminated its two top leaders, the after-effect could be a major shift of its political institutions.

At this juncture, the following factors would already be assumed:

- Egypt's agriculture and economy are ruined.
- The general population is in a state of shock and struggling to survive.
- King Tutankhamun is dead.
- The remaining Royal and government administrative personnel are non-responsive because they too, are in survival mode.
- Pharaoh Ay and his entire chariot army, having left to pursue after Moses and company, have completely disappeared.
- Any foreigners visiting Egypt at this time would observe the situation and could pass the information to other countries. This could be seen as an opportunity and trigger new military activity aimed at Egypt.

Given the fact that Pharaoh Ay had gone missing and unaccounted for, he obviously could not resume his role as Pharaoh. Was there anyone else around who could move into the gap and assume full control? Someone who was in a prominent position with real influence and access to *military power?*

Yes there was. His name was Horemheb and he was a person with the status and muscle to step in and assume control as the new Pharaoh. He was actually the commander and chief of the Egyptian army and also a top advisor during the reign of King Tut. He would have been perfectly poised to take over.

He was not part of Royal lineage either, but was a member of the inner administrative circles surrounding it. However, the incumbent good-old-boy network didn't have him in their back pocket.

With his new leadership role secured, his military power was used effectively to put down the resistance of the troublesome Armarna period.

After that, he successfully exercised his administrative abilities to restore stability in Egypt. With a loyal consortium in place to follow his orders, the expansion of his authority to outlying Egyptian territories would also happen and those would fall into line.

With that accomplished, the areas of agriculture and commerce were eventually restored to normal operation. His military position would have enabled him to rally whatever forces were left in order to maintain law and order and fend off threats. The dust settled and normal civilian life started to revive. However, some odious piles of dead frogs were probably still hanging around.

Although a country's religious institutions are not typically something that need restructuring after a major catastrophe, there was a lot of cleanup in this area that Horemheb took care of. The problem was a new monotheistic religious system that Akhenaten (formerly named Amenhotep 4) implemented for the worship of his sun god named Aten. He displaced the polytheistic religion that was the long-standing Egyptian standard and in so doing, upset much of the population.

Hmmm... I couldn't help but notice that the last part of Akhenaten's name ends with "aten." How about that for a coincidence huh?

Dinner conversations during this time went something like this:

> **Zahwi (father):** "I just learned that Akhenaten removed the great purple-speckled beetle god from the town square!"
>
> **Nileetah (mother):** "I heard that too! Someone told me that he also removed the great red-bellied salamander god!"
>
> **Billyhotep (son):** "My teacher at school told us that he removed the great yellow and green striped three-eyed flying wombat god from the central worship center!"
>
> **Zahwi (father):** Stands up from the dinner table in a fit of rage. "That's all I can take! We were supposed to go to the center next week for a flying wombat praise and worship service! This Akhenaten freak has got to go!!"

As for religious reforms, Horemheb, much to the relief of Egypt, demolished the monuments that had been installed by Akhenaten. He dismantled the temples that were dedicated to his sun god named Aten and used much of the building materials for new projects.

After making short work of that mess, Horemheb then re-instituted the traditional multi-god polytheistic religion of former Egypt.

If Ay drowned in the Red Sea, as I believe he did, then his vacancy would have allowed for a resistance-reduced setting that would have made things easier for Horemheb. He could execute his full takeover, and as history shows, this is exactly what happened.

Might almost-but-not-quite-yet "Pharaoh" Horemheb have sent out a scouting party to trace Ay's tracks and see what was going on? Perhaps.

But they would have followed the tracks from Succoth Egypt across the northern Sinai Peninsula to Etham (modern Elath), turned south through the mountain pass and then took an eastward jog up to the water's edge at Nuweiba beach, which is on the eastern leg of the Red Sea . . . and then what? There was simply nowhere else to go.

So with nothing but a bunch of chariot tracks and no chariots, the search party would have stopped right there, grabbed a bite to eat, packed it up and then returned home to give their report.[2]

Pharaoh Ay was about as stubborn as they get and arrogant to the max. He also might have taken his name, "Father of the God" a bit too seriously. A name like that could

---

[2] For more information on the Exodus, look up Ron Wyatt, *Revealing God's Treasures* DVD

elevate the holder to a rather lofty state of mind. This puts things in a clearer perspective, doesn't it?

The real God did give Ay plenty of opportunities to change his mind. There were more than enough miracles presented in order to get him to back off his hard-line stance.

Even Ay's own advisors told him to change his mind. Exodus 10:7 says "And Pharaoh's servants said unto him, How long shall this man be a snare unto us? Let the men go, that they may serve the Lord their God: knowest thou not yet that Egypt is destroyed?"

Ignoring nine plagues in a row is pretty bad. Ignoring the tenth plague of a supernatural carnage that left a death in every single Egyptian family is really bad.

But you'd think that when he pulled his chariot up to the Red Sea and observed the water parted and suspended right in place, he would have remembered what had just taken place back home. You'd think that he would have peered into the open gap to do a risk assessment and then figured it wasn't worth it.

Nope. Ay was not the type to take nay for an answer. So he and the boys decided to go for it and nudged the horses forward. I would guess that many of those in this chariot army knew it was a big mistake.

I can also imagine some of the aquatic creatures that were hanging out along the perimeter of the water walls.

Finster (shark #1): "Hey Bubbles! I think we've

got company!"
Bubbles (shark #2): "Yeah. Looks like Meals-On-Wheels! Call the gang!"
Finster: "Hey, the water walls are falling in. Let's go!"
Bubbles: "This is great! I was really getting tired of squid!"

You might take exception to the humor and the irony here. The thought of an entire army of men being drowned in this way is quite disturbing, isn't it? But there are two sides to every coin.

Exodus 1:15 says: "And the King of Egypt spoke unto the Hebrew midwives . . ."

Exodus 1:16 says: "And he said, When ye do the office of a midwife to the Hebrew women, and see them upon the stools; **if it be a son, then ye shall kill him**: but if it be a daughter, then she shall live."

Exodus 1:22 says: And Pharaoh charged all his people, saying, **Every son that is born ye shall cast into the river**, and every daughter ye shall save alive."

There were lots of alligators in the Nile river—most of them were hungry, too. And who do you think would have been rolling into town (Goshen) to check (raid) the households of the children of Israel in order to enforce their version of population control?

You guessed right: the Egyptian chariot brigade. What goes around comes around, so the saying goes.

Back in Egypt . . .
The scouting crew returned and gave their report. Pharaoh Ay, six hundred elite manned chariots and thousands of additional military personnel had vanished.

The field was now cleared of opposition and Horemheb took office. His reign was a lengthy one, running from 1319 to 1292 BC. This means he wasn't a flash in the pan. He had the qualifications to take control and keep it.

This is exactly the type of post-disaster government and civil "recovery" scenario that one would expect to see, given the circumstances.

It all makes perfect sense and therefore can be considered to substantiate the account of Passover, the Exodus and the Red Sea Crossing. It also helps to bolster the case for using "timeline" based methodology.

This is all some really incredible stuff. But it's much more than just a story. It's meant to be a story with a lesson that points us to "something."

Let's move on to take a closer look at the Red Sea Crossing and how this miraculous event mirrors a future prophetic event called the Rapture.

11

Correlation Between the Red Sea Crossing and the Rapture

This account in Exodus has a miraculous outcome that seems to prophetically mirror the church-Rapture narrative.

Egyptian bondage—a picture of the Church in the world
The children of Israel were being held as slave labor in Egypt. God wanted to get his children back home where they belonged. God sent Moses from his current abode of 40 years (in Midian) back to Egypt in order to get them out. Egypt adamantly resisted this directive from God so God sent ten plagues to help them change their minds.

The first Passover—a picture of Christ the Lamb of God
God had Moses instruct the children of Israel to observe the Passover so that they could avoid the last plague, which would be death. Those who obeyed were basically . . . passed over.

Those who did not obey suffered the tenth plague. They were not passed over. The sacrificing of the Passover Lamb with the application of its blood was able to save those who obeyed this command.

The Exodus—the Church distancing itself from the world

Moses led the children of Israel out of Egypt and towards the place that He determined was best for them. The journey was not easy and there were trials and testing along the way.

The Red Sea Crossing—the Church is miraculously rescued

The children of Israel were out of Egypt but not quite out of danger. The situation reached a climax as the enemy closed in. God miraculously opened a door for the children of Israel to pass through to safety and then closed the door on the enemy.

The Correlation—God's strategy revealed

The idea that Passover itself is *the switch* that immediately turns on the *Rapture light* is probably not correct.

This pre-miracle event, though absolutely essential in that it included the blood of a sacrificial lamb (the blood of Christ - the Lamb of God), did not constitute a clean break "from" and transition "to" the place where God wanted them to be.

What it did actually do was give God's children a special identity mark (passport) for them to have in their possession for when the time of a miraculous departure was divinely scheduled.

The Red Sea Crossing has a uniquely "miraculous escape" attribute quality that is also found in the description of the Rapture. This is the actual supernatural component that needs to be realized as the correct correlation.

Note: the journey on foot (two hundred miles or so) that Israel made from Succoth Egypt to Nuweiba beach in Israel could be done in seven days. Moses and Israel would have had to keep a brisk and steady pace to achieve this journey but it's quite achievable. This seven-day physical journey time-span is celebrated in the Feast of Passover, which also happens to last seven days.

The point of this analysis is to present a good reason for citing Passover as the preferred time-frame marker in which a departure passport will come into play.

The seven-day Passover feast of 2021 may possibly bring a surprise-ending miracle that is prophetically reminiscent of the Red Sea crossing miracle.

Rapture "typology" options: Passover / Red Sea Crossing versus The Feast of Trumpets

This now brings us to a part of the study where there are differing points of view regarding which Biblical typology works best for representing the Rapture.

Does the strength of the typology offered by the Passover / Red Sea Crossing outweigh the strength of the Feast of Trumpets? Which of the two proposals is the best one?

The Passover / Red Sea Crossing event closely resembles the Christian experience in the world and its hope of leaving to be with God some day.

The Feast of Trumpets has a very clear "trumpet" connotation about it. The reference to the word trumpet is found in Corinthians and Thessalonians. But the trumpet proposal is mostly an assertion that the physical act of blowing a shofar is what makes it a good candidate.

Historically, the blowing of the shofar was used to alert the military to gather for war, proclaim a victory over an enemy, announce the Sabbaths, festivals or other significant events. The trumpet call does the job in these situations.

But in the Rapture call scenario, the trumpet call is just the **third and last part** of the total multi-part audible annunciation given by the Lord to the Church. The first two parts cannot be overlooked. They carry the weight with regards to priority in terms of their "linguistic" nature.

The **first part** was literally the voice of Jesus giving a shout.

The **second part** was the voice of the archangel.

I would think that the actual voice of GOD and the voice of the Archangel that precede the trumpet blasts would negate the idea that the initiation of the Rapture depends solely on the trumpet sound.

Since the astronomical factor is a big part of this book and worthy of serious consideration, I want to fortify the argument for Passover with the added fact of the Lunar Tetrads. They clearly have Passover on the billboard as number one.

So with this information, I would be strongly inclined

towards the Passover/Red Sea Crossing "typology" as the better of the two choices.

A bit of extra information about the miracle of the Red Sea Crossing: Documented artifacts and recorded video of coral encrusted chariot wheels being found on the bottom of the Red Sea from off the coast of Nuweiba beach continuing over to the other side (Saudi Arabia) are available for anyone to learn about and see.

A man named Ron Wyatt made this amazing discovery in 1978. God has intentionally left physical evidence for the entire world to examine in order to demonstrate to us that He does perform miracles. There have also been other documentaries of this same discovery that confirm the validity of the evidence.

Question: Why did God so precisely intersperse the historical timeline with a string of prophetic event markers? Here's the best straightforward answer that I can come up with:

- God is the Creator and He has a plan.
- God said that He created mankind in His image.
- God wants His created image (mankind) to follow His plan.
- God graciously placed markers in His plan to guide mankind along the way.

Furthermore, the events of the Passover, Exodus and Red Sea Crossing are intended to demonstrate a divine initiative that says God will get his children out of wherever they are to a new place where he wants them to be.

This information reinforces the Passover-Exodus-Red Sea Crossing as a good timeline marker at the midpoint of timeline chart.

12

THE MIRACLE OF THE RAPTURE

This is an extremely difficult subject to cover. I've tried my best to break it down into several sub-categories and step through each in detail.

Here's a very short and plain paraphrase of what the Apostle Paul describes: "Christians will be removed (beamed up) clean off the planet Earth."

Paul apparently got the details about the Rapture event (caught up) directly from Jesus (1st Thessalonians 4:15). There's no possible way that Paul, as brilliant as he was, could have invented such a wild "supernatural" concept.

John the Revelator was also informed of this same supernatural event when in Revelation Chapter 12, he used the word "harpazo." This is the *exact* same word (harpazo) used by Paul. Though his version is not phrased in the same manner as Paul, the fact of these two apostles bringing this incredible concept to light serves to provide corroboration of this prophetic future event.

Regarding those believers who heard this incredible information, the only way that the conveyance of such a supernatural concept could be accepted as truth was if it was already understood that the source of this information(Jesus Christ) was in fact, supernatural.

Those hearing this information were already aware of the supernatural realm because all of them knew about the supernatural resurrection of Jesus. They were also well aware of the resurrection of Lazarus prior to that. The First Advent of Emmanuel (God with us) shattered their ordinary mundane lives with miracle after miracle after miracle, which illuminated their minds to the reality of the supernatural.

It is documented (Luke 24 and Acts 4:3) that Jesus, after he was resurrected, spent considerable time (forty days) with the apostles, their families and friends. During that time, Jesus would have had plenty of time to expound on the scriptures and strengthen their faith.

Spiritual reinforcement was something that God planned for in advance. The account of Jesus meeting the two disciples on the road to Emmaus is the proof.

What is amazing is that the Emmaus road teaching session happened on the very *first day* (Luke 24:13) of the resurrection!

Is God interested in helping both our faith and prophetic *knowledge* to increase? Yes, He certainly is. The teaching sessions given by Jesus to his disciples did include insight into immediate future events, for example the destruction of Jerusalem in 70 AD, and also "last days" (end-times) events.

The establishment of Christ's kingdom on Earth was already something that they had anticipated and hoped for. But now they would have been able to learn about it with the understanding of God's long-range plan for building the Church.

It is also quite probable that the mysterious topic of the harpazo event was explained to them. They would have known full well that they were not going to experience being caught up. This event was determined for a future generation.

It was after all these events were concluded that the kingdom was finally going to be set up. Paul was able to reassure them of this fact in his epistles.

Purpose for the Rapture

It states in Genesis 1 that God created the world and everything else contained therein. That would make Him the owner of the property.

Recall the parable (Luke 29:9-16) about the property owner who takes a journey and leaves his property with workers to take care of it. They didn't do a very good job and the owner eventually came back to reckon with them. The reckoning process was most likely not very pleasant.

This parable has the planet Earth and its occupants (mankind) in mind. There are two main responsibilities that were given to the occupants.

Those responsibilities would be obeying God's commands and maintaining the planet in good condition. That means the land, the sea, the air and all life forms.

By the looks of things, the property is overdue for a complete restoration. Before that work can begin, some valuable items are going to be removed so they don't get damaged in the process. This would be the purpose for the Rapture.

The teaching by the Apostle Paul says that God is going to supernaturally remove his children (his followers = Christians) off the planet and keep them safe from His coming judgment (reckon = wrath) that is called the Great Tribulation.

Later in 1st Thessalonians 5:9 Paul says "For God hath not appointed us to wrath." God plans to remove His children from wrath (judgment).

An example of divine judgment on a large-scale would be the account of the Flood and Noah's Ark in Genesis 6. The world's majority population provoked God's wrath. Noah and his family were spared.

The theme of divine consequences for the disobedient and compassion for the obedient runs continuously from Genesis to Revelation. It's impossible to miss this concept. The Rapture is consistent with this theme.

Paul is basically telling the Thessalonian Christians that there is a future time of large-scale judgment (wrath) coming and it's not appointed (intended) for them.

English phrase "caught up" is the Greek word "harpazo"
The English phrase found in the Bible "caught up" is translated from the original Greek word *harpazo*. This word is unmistakable. The word "Rapture" is the commonly used

reference. "Caught up" (*harpazo*) occurs in just two places in the New Testament.

It's very probable that the Apostle Paul and the Apostle John would have had discussions with each other about this amazing topic and thus *harpazo* is used by both of them.

First, Paul uses it in 1st Thessalonians 4:17: "Then we which are alive and remain will be **caught up** . . ." Second, John uses it in Revelation 12:5: "and her child was **caught up** unto God . . ."

In both cases, the Greek word *harpazo* describes the event as a very sudden and extremely fast removal of the church. The words "immediate evacuation" are also very applicable. This is sort of a rescue operation that takes place.

In the caught-up scenario (1 Thes 4:16), Jesus "descends from heaven with a shout, with the voice of the archangel, and with the trump of God" (audible) and the event is initiated. This is amazing because it would have to encompass the entire globe.

The raising of the "dead in Christ" (bodies reunited with their spirits) takes place first. Immediately after that, the Rapture of living Christians takes place. Both groups are gathered together as one complete group in the heavens (upper atmosphere) above.

In 1st Corinthians 15:51, Paul says "Behold, I show you a mystery; we shall all not sleep, but we shall all be changed."

Conclusion: The mystery is revealed. The living saints will not die but be supernaturally transformed.

Verse 52: "In a moment, in the twinkling of an eye, at the last trump: for the trumpet shall sound, and the dead shall be raised incorruptible, and we shall be changed."

Conclusion: The event happens suddenly and extremely fast. The very last blast of the trumpet is the one that actually turns the key. The bodies of dead saints are raised and transformed into new perfect immortal beings and the living saints are also raised (caught up) and transformed into new perfect immortal beings.

The amazing supernatural aspect and the post Rapture scenario

This section is extremely difficult to cover. If I could talk to Paul, I'd say something like: "Paul, the Greek texts are great and our linguistic experts did the very best they could to interpret but, do you have any video footage lying around?"

In 1st Thes 4:17, the verse explains that Christians will be "caught up together with them in the **clouds**, to meet the Lord in the **air**." The exact altitude is absent from this statement, which leaves room for conjecture.

Let's look carefully at the literal interpretation.

The words "clouds" and "air" (Strong's Concordance #3507 and #109) mean that this caught up area is way *up there* above street-level but not way *out there* beyond the stratosphere.

Strong's #3507 = "cloud"
Strong's #109 = "(to breathe) air"

The text also doesn't say "out in the vacuum of space". Human beings need to breathe in order to live, and that means oxygen. Paul didn't give any indication that oxygen bottles would be passed out either. The gaseous oxygenated layer that surrounds the planet Earth is what is actually implied here.

What about the actual place where the Christians go up to? Is it a landing zone of some kind? What would it be made of?

I can only speculate here. It could be a temporary canopy or shell up near the clouds. It would have to be solid or dense enough to bear up an extremely large number of people and would also cover a substantial portion of the circumference of the globe. Seeing as we're talking about an enormous area and the Earth is round, the shape of this thing would obviously be curved. This would of course be 100% supernatural in the event of its instantaneous creation.

I'm guessing that this supernatural staging area or "shell" would be around 10,000 feet or so in elevation but not too high where the air is too thin to breath. This is basically the uppermost level with oxygen or the troposphere.

I've heard some people claim that the Rapture will instantaneously transport the church to a heavenly abode located billions and trillions and zillions of miles away. But that claim is pure fantasy that cannot be justified anywhere in scripture. The information that Paul gives does *not* indicate that amount of distance being traveled.

In my opinion, there's got to be a continuation of traffic flow. This aerial staging area would be cluttering up the skies and susceptible to danger of some kind.

We all know that air travel (civilian and military) would certainly qualify as a potential risk. But during such a miraculous event, all civilian air traffic would probably be grounded temporarily. Only military aircraft would be allowed to fly but I'm confident that God would prevent any mishaps.

There is another possible risk factor that is described in the Book of Revelation that does fit this scenario. It has an almost science fiction quality to it, but it really needs to be approached in a true-to-form, "that's just what it says" manner.

After the Church (the restrainer = the elect) has been vacated via the Rapture, there's a shift in focus to other incredible activities that occur in outer space and then afterwards on the planet Earth.

Rev 12:7 "And there was war in heaven: Michael and his angels fought against the dragon; and the dragon fought and his angels,"

Rev 12:8: "And prevailed not; neither was their place found any more in heaven."

Rev 12:9: "And the great dragon was cast out, that old

serpent, called the Devil, and Satan, which deceiveth the whole world: **he was cast out into the world and his angels were cast out with him.**"

Revelation is describing an end-times war in heaven (outer space) that involves God's angelic forces fighting against and Satan's angelic forces.

Angels conducting warfare in outer space? How does that work?? Let's first realize that God created these special beings with abilities and powers that are in many ways beyond human. They have these abilities because they routinely operate in manner that is beyond normal human capability.

Consider an account in scripture where one particularly powerful angelic being had some serious warfare to conduct.

2 Kings 19:35 says "And it came to pass that night, that the angel of the Lord went out, and smote in the camp of the Assyrians an hundred fourscore and five thousand: and when they arose early in the morning, behold they were all dead corpses." That's *one* angel destroying an entire army of 185,000 soldiers in *one* night. No contest, done deal.

But these special created angelic beings are like us in many ways. They have form. They think. They know good from bad. They eat. They drink. They travel. They can communicate verbally. They also breathe the same air that we do.

But they have an edge: they routinely travel the cosmos.

In Ezekiel (Ez 1:1-28) there is a very detailed description of what many believe (myself included) to be a super-high-tech vehicle that was used (past and present) for transportation of heavenly beings, including angels.

I'm going to theorize that angels breathe air *all of the time* and they require an environment that *always has it.*

I'm also going to theorize that the vehicle that Ezekiel described (Ezek 1) had an interior with an intricate system that could produce an environment suitable for sustaining beings that need to breathe air.

Ezekiel also described this vehicle as it performed some maneuvers. It was not stationary for the entire time that he observed it. It's reasonable to conclude that for the vehicle to move, it had to have some kind of system for propulsion. No, not jet propulsion via fuel as our aircraft use today, but something quite different. For lack of a better term we'll call it "very advanced technology."

I believe that this information was recorded in the Book of Ezekiel to help us (who are of a future generation) to understand a bit about the realm of outer space. God gives us a small glimpse into this area. The rest of it we have to speculate about.

I mean, how did you think the angels actually travel from Heaven to Earth and back again? Do they flap their angelic wings to take off and then just before they hit the vacuum of space, they take a deep breath and hold it in? Nonsense. They have "very advanced technology" and they've had it for a very long time.

In ancient Biblical terminology, Ezekiel was describing "heavenly powers" comprised of elements including a cloud, fire that in-folds itself, wings, wheels in the midst of wheels and brightness about it. Those were the words he used.

"Spacecraft" was simply not part of the lexicon in those days. The terminology he used was the very best that was available at that time to make sense of it.

The latter part of Ez 1:20 says ". . .and the wheels were lifted up over against them: for the spirit of the living creature was in the wheels."

What Ezekiel is seeing is a craft of some kind that moves, but he can't see what it is that's actually propelling it. The mysterious force (advanced technology) that is causing this thing to move is unseen and thus the word "spirit" is used.

What in the world could compare with such an incredible futuristic craft?

Our cars. They move here and they move there. The wheels turn and the body goes right along with them as they turn. But you can't see what is making it all move even though they all move in unison. There's an unseen chassis involved and the engine (power source) is hidden under the hood, out of view.

The only reason that we can now accurately call out "very advanced technology" is because we ourselves have technology (flight) that has advanced to a level high enough whereby we can recognize some of the signature characteristics.

It's apparent that the good angelic beings have a form of highly advanced transportation as described by Ezekiel. We can also assume from Rev 12:9 that these vehicles have the ability to engage in battle and use on-board weaponry to shoot and destroy. And I'm guessing that they don't miss their targets either. Listen up folks . . . lasers have been around for decades . . . ho hum.

What type of vehicles would the angelic beings (both the good and the bad) use to fly around in outer space and in the immediate space (high or low) that surrounds our planet?

I don't know. Let's just say that their vehicles are "unidentified" and leave it at that.

I know that the information that I'm putting forth here may be too difficult to fully grasp. It's not a walk in the park, as they say. But I really hope that you didn't purchase this book hoping to read a cute little sermonette built on a three-point outline.

Continuing now (Rev 12:9) with the angels doing battle in outer space.

The war continues and then ends with Satan and his demonic angels being forced down to the surface of the planet Earth. God also stops Satan's forces from being able to travel any more in outer space.

At this point they are stationed or "fixed" on planet Earth with no way off.

What do you think they're going to be doing, now that

they find themselves stuck on the planet Earth?

That's right. They're going to do what they do best: make trouble, or "tribulation."

Rev 12:7-9 is a certainly real eye opener. Who could possibly imagine such a thing as warfare being conducted in outer space huh? Maybe somebody should take the idea and make a movie about it. Maybe they'll call the movie "Galaxy Something" or "Star Something." It could be a big box-office hit!

Anyway, this type of angelic war activity would definitely pose a threat to those people waiting on the staging area shell up in the clouds. Thus they would need to be moved off the shell in order to avoid being impacted by that war.

Back to the staging area shell: there's a massive group of people waiting.

Where could such a mass of people go from there? The Rapture-caught up scenario is transitional and there must be more to it than just "poof . . . gone."

Beyond the staging area there's nowhere to go but outer space. What type of transfer method or equipment would be used to move millions of people off the atmospheric shell? Does God even need equipment? He should be able to simply think it and make it happen, right?

Without going any further, it has to be understood that this is still 100% in the realm of the supernatural. God would still be in total control of everything here.

I'm going to pass on speculating about the type of

transfer method and if any equipment would be used. I honestly have no idea.

But this study is very seriously and logically attempting to analyze an event scenario called the Rapture. At this point it has to be understood that a Rapture event has indeed happened and there must be a progression from the staging area to "somewhere."

What are some options for an area or place that could accommodate millions of people after a transfer had been done and the staging shell has been removed?

Such a place would have to be absolutely enormous, geo-physically stable, have a gravitational field, oxygen supply, fresh water supply, a huge stockpile of provisions and enough accommodations or "housing" to put all the people in.

What in the world could do *all that?* Well, we just happen to have a very good example of a working model that's been around for a long time, the planet Earth. It has all of the above listed features and much more.

Could another, similar planet be able to accept the transfer of millions or more post-Rapture people? Possibly. Many in the past have postulated similar questions.

But to the best of my knowledge there is no documented evidence of it. At least, those of us who don't own a Hubble telescope don't have any proof. Only those who have "first-in-line" exclusive priority access to photographic and video records of other interesting celestial bodies would know.

But if they actually had such planetary information, they probably wouldn't be too quick to let the cat out of the bag. It would be highly classified information that the public doesn't need know due to the sensitive nature of the subject and the possibility of panic.

Let's check out John 14:2-3 for some info.

John 14:2 says "In my Father's house are many mansions: if it were not so, I would have told you. I go to prepare a place for you."

This tells us that the Father's house (residence) has (present tense) many mansions. In other words, it currently exists as an *established* place and has many large homes that are built and occupied.

John 14:3 says "And if I go and prepare a place for you, I will come again, and receive you unto myself; that where I am, there ye may be also."

This tells us that Jesus will be leaving to prepare (future tense) a *new* place. In other words, Jesus is leaving to prepare a "new place" and will be returning back to Earth with this "new place" to bring (transfer) his people to this new place so that they can be together with him. I'm assuming that this new place has many newly built large homes that are ready to accept new occupants.

Verse 14:3 gives us some more extremely important information. When he says, "receive you", he's talking about *his* people (Christians) who are currently living on planet Earth.

The word "receive" here implies that the Christians are

moving or traveling into the presence of Jesus when he returns and not the other way around.

Strong's concordance (#3880) defines "receive" as "to receive near." There's a cross reference to SC #2983 where we find an alternate tense defined as "to take" or "to get hold of." There's even an additional stronger tense that is defined as "take (away up)." These definitions help to make the picture very clear.

With the word "receive" properly interpreted, it looks like John 14:3 supports my theory. Remember, in order for my theory to work there are two factors involved that must conform to the Biblical narrative. First is the question of mobility from and to, and the word "receive" works properly. Second is the question of location and capacity, and the words "new place" work properly.

The theory again: There's a post-Rapture transfer of Christians that moves them "off and up" from the staging area shell to a new place that has many mansions (or large homes) that are finished-built and awaiting the arrival of new occupants.

All that's left to do is figure out what that new place might be. Without any hesitation or fear, I'm going to boldly go where no man has gone before!

I'm going to propose that the new "place that has been prepared" by God, that has plenty of "mansions", is actually a planet. Considering the scale involved, this concept works well.

There's a little something in the Book of Revelation

(mostly overlooked) that surprisingly lends credence to my theory. In Rev 7:9, John is looking at a large group of martyred tribulation saints in his Heavenly vision. There are so many that he can't begin to count them all.

Read Rev 7:9: "After this I beheld, and, lo, a great multitude, which no man could number, of all nations, and kindreds, and people, and tongues, stood before the throne, and before the Lamb, clothed with white robes, and palms in their hands".

In this verse it says that John sees an extremely large group of people who happen to be holding "palms" (palm branches) in their hands.

Now here's a question that you may think rather strange but it does lead somewhere. Do you think God would supply everyone with plastic palm branches?

Answer: No, they're not plastic. They're real.

So we've got a lot of real palm branches and they're just begging to answer some questions.

Let's proceed to the questions...

1) So they must have been cut from real palm trees, right?

2) And because such a huge amount of real palm branches have been distributed to all these people, we can assume that there's a sufficient amount of real palm trees growing in order to supply them, right?

3) And these trees would naturally require air, light and water, right?

4) And real palm trees have root systems that are typically found growing in something called "soil", right?

5) And soil happens to be the typical nutrient rich top layer on the surface of all "dry-land continents", right?

6) And dry-land continents are typically found on the surface area of something called a "planet", right?

That's right... a PLANET.

And after all, our current existing working model (a planet that was expertly designed and implemented by God) provides a suitable environment whereby a wide variety of plant life (including palm trees) can flourish. I figure that His original design works so well then why not stick with it... simple.

And why palm branches specifically? Could there be any possible symbolism involved here? Yes, there is.

In regards to the First Advent when Jesus was approaching Jerusalem as King and was greeted by the locals, John 12:13 says: "Took branches of palm trees, and went forth to meet him, and cried, Hosanna: Blessed is the King of Israel that cometh in the name of the Lord." This is a form of acknowledging the entry of Royalty onto the scene and laying out a welcome mat.

Palm branches have also been assigned significance as the Easter celebration begins with Palm Sunday. God, the creator of palm trees thought highly enough of this beautiful tree to designate its branches to be used in honoring The Son of God, who was later resurrected on Resurrection Sunday. Anything terrestrial or celestial is His to utilize for His glory and even more so as this special celebration intersects exactly with Passover.

Additionally, the people of Rev 7:9 waving the palm branches are probably fully aware that they are part of the triumphal entry (or re-entry) of Jesus back to planet earth for His Second Advent. There surely has been a lot of information conveyed to them as to where they are, what has happened and what's going to happen soon. After all, John says that they were before the throne (stationed in an organized gathering) with Jesus, the elders and the angels so there would have been plenty of advance communication. This display of palm branches also hints to a sense of imminent expectation. I'm guessing that it's an expectation of an impending arrival to their destination.

Let's briefly touch on one important side note. God doesn't need a planet and He doesn't need oxygen. He is the Creator of all things. He is Spirit and eternal. He pre-existed this particular 6000-plus year segment of time in which planet earth and mankind (human beings) were made. But this unique and very special part of His creation was predetermined to have (as an integral living component) the actual physical manifest presence of God the Son in human form. So in taking on a human form, He also subjected Himself to a variety of circumstances within an earthly (planetary) realm.

So I'm theorizing that it's another actual literal planet that's in play here.

Seeing as it would have to sustain all the saints of the past and also have enough extra room to take on and sustain this new group (a great multitude which no man could number), I'm guessing that this planet is several times larger than planet Earth. Consider this... our planetary model has been in operation for 6000 plus years so it would makes sense that the other planet has experienced a steady increase in its occupancy rate. And God did say that there were many mansions and that would have to equate to a vast amount of real estate. So I'm confident that He's got it all worked out as well as the future plan for expansion that extends far beyond the Millennium and eternity.

If you are the least bit aware of how history seems to be leading us "somewhere", and how divine involvement is evident in the circumstances, then you've got your nose in the right place (book). You're curious. You're thinking. You may even be sensing a sort of "clock's-a-ticking" feeling and you simply don't want to be caught off guard and left in the dark. That could very well be a directed spiritual inclination that you should not ignore. That's exactly what I have been experiencing (and I suspect others also) and that's why the concept of divine long-range planning is what stuck in my mind when methodically building the timeline chart found in later in this book.

Let's get back to the planet.

I'm thinking of giving this planet a name. All the current planets have been given names so this planet should get a name too. Seeing as how the Rapture theme has the idea of leaving or exit, I'm going to call it Planet Exit.

According to John 14:3, the Planet Exit would have to have Jesus Christ already stationed on it because "where I am, there ye may be also."

Planet Exit would probably be arriving at a distance from Earth that is close enough to allow for the transfer of people from the staging area, but not too close as to crash. God knows that rocking the boat here would be catastrophic.

But on the other hand, a bit of "boat-rocking" could be the causal reason for the type of cataclysmic events that are described in the Great Tribulation.

Isaiah 24:19 says "The earth is utterly broken down, the earth is clean dissolved, **the earth is moved exceedingly**."

Isaiah 24:20 says "The **earth shall reel to and fro like a drunkard**, and shall be removed like a cottage; and the transgression thereof shall be heavy upon it; and it shall fall, and shall not rise again."

But how could Planet Exit approach this area, do a taxi quick stop, pick up the passengers and then drive away? Planets don't have brakes.

Answer: Planet Exit could simply follow an established orbital path that comes close enough in spatial proximity to planet Earth to do a rolling stop. This would minimize the travel distance at the optimal point of intersection. The transporting of the passengers (saints) from off the staging area shell to the new "prepared place" could be done.

According to the scriptures, the Great Tribulation lasts three and a half years and then concludes with Jesus Christ Messiah returning to planet Earth with his saints. This means Planet Exit would have to reverse course and go back.

The total orbital segment of Planet Exit at the time of its passenger pickup to the time of its arrival back, at that exact same place of intersection with planet Earth, would have to equal three and a half years.

That means that the orbital "first-approach" segment would last 1 year and 9 months and the "second-approach" segment would last 1 year and 9 months.

What would be the place along the orbital path where Planet Exit performs a loop-around? That place would have to be the sun in our solar system.

Isn't that suggesting that Planet Exit is part of our solar system? Yes, it is only "suggesting" and that is all. Remember, I did preface this section by saying that "the new place" explanation was going to be difficult.

The only way that this theory could gain serious credibility would be if several or more amateur astronomers were to discover and simultaneously report a new and "very bright" planetary body that's gradually getting bigger as it approaches. Such a discovery would have to happen sometime in late 2020 to early 2021.

But the NASA folks might be leaving their lens caps on for that event. After all, the consensus from all of the world's major observatories is that this mysterious bright object is nothing more than a stray high-altitude weather balloon! ☺ "Nothing to see here folks. Move along . . . move along."

Anyway, if such an observation were actually made, many people with an open mind towards prophetic astronomical signs would finally get some satisfaction.

The signs in the sun, moon and stars (Luke 21:25) would finally have their day of reckoning. To the observers on Earth, it would be a shocking . . . revelation. The occurrence of a first-approach sighting followed by an actual "caught up" event would then certify the information from Paul and John as a true fact.

Bit by bit, the post-Rapture/post tribulation homecoming scenario is hopefully starting to come into view. The theory I'm proposing does have some science behind it to back it up.

But just to officially cover all the bases, the prophesy of Zechariah 14:1-4 makes it absolutely clear that Jesus is physically returning to Planet Earth and more specifically the Mount of Olives in Jerusalem. That is exactly what it says and in so doing, it would have to be describing the literal "Second Advent."

The return leg (1 year and 9 months) of Planet Exit's journey would of course require another rolling-stop deal for the passengers (saints) led by Jesus Christ (Rev 19:14-19) to disembark. This would be the literal Second Advent.

This entire group would be returning to planet Earth to

a place called Armageddon. And it's a total war zone, not a beachfront resort.

Could the two 1-year and 9 month "in close" orbital segments (three and a half years total) help to calculate a definitive total orbit for Planet Exit?

Probably not. It only *suggests* that this loop-around portion of the orbital path could be a small part of a much larger elliptical orbit. But given the fact that the "designer" of this system chose a central core (sun) with surrounding objects attached or secured to it via gravitational fields, the concept is in harmony with the design.

I have no absolute hard data on the gravity field for the suggested Planet Exit orbit. But we do know that the planet Pluto is *way, way out there* and it's still orbiting as usual, despite riding the extreme perimeter.

My theory for Planet Exit, though somewhat radical, still has merit because it works reasonably well within a pre-existing functional system or model, our very own solar system.

If you think my concept is too incredible to believe, I've got another one for you.

1st Kings 17:1-6 describes when Elijah was on the run from Ahab with no food to eat. God commanded some ravens (verse 6) to bring him bread and meat for breakfast and dinner. Who would have believed that a bunch of ravens could run a kosher deli with free delivery! This happens to be the very first recorded use of drone delivery service.

Well, hopefully this logical-technical analysis of the Rapture topic will help in gaining some practical understanding.

The Rapture is intended for the Children of the Light / Day

Reference the Book of 1st Thessalonians by the Apostle Paul. What I'm looking for in this epistle by Paul is something that indicates an order of events. It's already understood who the people groups are, but it's the presence of an actual "sequence" that will help to support the timeline chart. In order to be thorough, I'm going to run down all the pertinent verses. This section uses the Bible as the source material so that is essentially what determines the context.

Paul makes two main distinctions in this section:

- There are two groups described and those are the "Children of Light" and the "Children of Darkness."

- The "Children of Light" are Raptured before the "Children of Darkness" receive wrath.

1st Thes 4:17: "Then we which are alive and remain shall be caught up (*harpazo*) together with them in the clouds, to meet the Lord in the air: and so shall we ever be with the Lord."

The word "we" (Thes 4:17) that Paul uses is referring to Christians because he is specifically addressing the "church" in the town of Thessalonica.

The caught up (*harpazo*) event is clearly equated with a

vertical (upwardly) trip to meet the Lord (Jesus Christ) in the air above the Earth's surface.

This brief trip eventuates in a new and permanent location change that is situated in the literal presence (physical proximity) to Jesus Christ himself.

1st Thes 5:1-2: "But of the times and seasons, brethren, ye have no need that I write unto you. For yourselves know perfectly that the day of the Lord so cometh as a thief in the night."

Paul states that the time frame for the Rapture is not a new mystery for them because Paul himself already previously informed them of this. This is simply a refresher course. What also needs to be understood here is that the Lord is coming as a "thief", or unexpectedly.

1st Thes 5:3: "then sudden destruction cometh upon them . . . and they shall not escape."

Conclusion: The word "then" means that the destruction comes *after* the events of previous verse have transpired.

1st Thes 5:4: "but ye brethren are not in darkness that that day should overtake you as a thief."

Conclusion: The Christian brethren are not oblivious to the *approaching time* of the Rapture. They won't be caught off guard.

1st Thes 5:5: "ye are all children the light, and the children of the day: we are not of the night, nor of the darkness."

Conclusion: There's an evident contrast between God's

children of the light (day) and those who are of the night (darkness).

1st Thes 5:6: "Therefore let us not sleep as others, but let us watch and be sober"

Conclusion: The Christian brethren need to be alert, watchful and serious about the "times and seasons," mentioned in verse 2.

What are the times and seasons mentioned in verse 2? They are the end-times warnings from Jesus in Matthew 24 and Luke 21.

1st Thes 5:9: "For God hath not **appointed** us to **wrath** . . ."

The word "appointed" here means that God has determined something (wrath) to happen and it will surely happen. The target for the appointed wrath is *not* the "children of the day" but rather the "children of the dark."

Because Paul, as evidenced by his writings, advanced his arguments by stepping though in a logical manner, it's likely that what he is saying is the "children of the day" will be gone *before* the "children of the dark" are to receive the wrath (judgment). That is the apparent sequence.

This sequence is consistent with the harpazo-tribulation pattern that is found in the Book of Revelation 12:5-6.

With this informationfrom Paul, we also have more data that supports the timeline chart.

Reference the Book of Revelation and Ezekiel. Now let's consider the wrath of God in the "Time of Jacob's Trouble."

But don't forget, although this terrible time on Earth has the nation of Israel as the main target, the entire world (top to bottom) will be coming under severe catastrophic judgment.

Rev 8:13: "...Woe, Woe, Woe to the **inhabiters of the earth** . . .". That means every person on the globe will be affected.

With regard to prophetic geography, in order for a Great Tribulation or the "time of Jacob's trouble" to occur, it presupposes that there *is* an actual Jacob (country of Israel—ref. Ezekiel 37) in existence to experience the "trouble." That has been a reality since 1948.

To further cement Jacob's existence into place and certify Ezekiel 37, Jerusalem was restored to Israel as its capital in 1967 (Six Day War) and has remained in that state ever since. I'm not going to elaborate on the border-politics for that particular region. I'm simply pointing out the reality of the geography.

The end-time prophesies of the Rapture and the Second Advent come into sharper focus as we see more of the puzzle pieces of that middle-east region being put together.

As far as the smaller puzzle pieces, there's a Jerusalem. There's a temple mount and a Mount of Olives. There's also plenty of solid archeological evidence to validate the Biblical history of that area.

As far as the friction that is ongoing in that entire region (see Psalm 83), I'm just going to point out that this situation has been escalating recently to the point where it's not a small skirmish. It's clearly on the brink of war. I'm not going to run down the list of antagonists because there are already many other sources that go into great detail on that subject. But this escalation surely indicates a ramp-up to a much higher level of tension that could easily fuel a Great Tribulation period.

The Great Tribulation is described as lasting for three and a half years in three different ways using "time/s and a half", "months" and "days." These time-span verses are all appropriately located in "last-days / end-time" sections of prophesy and it's by design.

Here are the verses:

Daniel 8:25, "time, times and the dividing of times"
Daniel 12:7, "time, times and a half"
Rev 11:2, "forty two months"
Rev 11:3, "thousand two hundred threescore days"
Rev 12:6, "thousand two hundred threescore days"
Rev 12:14, "time, times and a half"

There's lots of confusion out there about the subject of the Great Tribulation but the verses listed above are very clear. The Great Tribulation lasts three and a half years, not seven years. It is actually Daniels seventieth week that has a time span duration of seven years.

If the seventieth week can be approximated on the timeline chart and the Great Tribulation situated to cover the last half of that time span, then the Rapture might find its placement just before that, somewhere around the midpoint of the timeline chart.

The Rapture event as described by the Apostle Paul and John is absolutely amazing. If it weren't for the fact of all the detailed information that went into their discourse on the subject, one would find it impossible to fathom.

The surrounding events, scenarios and technology that I've attempted to explain are also quite amazing. But they do have a basis in the scriptures, even if they're out on the fringes of traditional thought.

I would not have attempted to build the new walls if there wasn't already a solid foundation in place.

13

Rapture Found in Revelation 12

Revelation 12 is a broad overview of Biblical history but with an astronomical correlation and symbolism that perfectly illustrates the Biblical story. It starts off with the "great wonder in heaven" (very important sign) that the Apostle John saw.

In reading thorough Revelation 12, verses 1 and 2, the story of a woman (Mary [Israel] = Virgo) and the birth of Christ are clearly seen.

Moving forward in verses 3 and 4, the red dragon (Satan [Herod] = Draco) appears and threatens to devour her child as soon as it's born.

Next in verse 5 comes a picture of Jesus Christ as King of Kings and Lord of Lords over the entire planet. With Him will be His Church who will rule with Him.

Verse 5: "And she brought forth a man child who was to rule all nations with a rod of iron: and her child was caught up to God, and to his throne."

The "she" in this verse speaks about the nation of Israel that produced Messiah. The "child" refers to the spiritual offspring or byproducts of Messiah, which were His children, otherwise known as the Assembly (ecclesia) or the Church.

The combination "man child" phrase can be explained in this way: when Jesus Christ ("man") is combined with or integrates his children ("child"), the resulting collective Christian church body is "man child."

But there's also something interesting showing up in the latter part of verse 5.

The words "caught up" (*harpazo*) is used in relation to the "child" that the woman brought forth. It says "and **her child was caught up** to God, and to his throne." The word "man" is not included here. Only the word "child" is used.

There's a very plausible explanation for this. The child (Church) named in verse 5 has been Raptured.

In Strong's Concordance (#730 - Greek = *arsen*) is the word "man" and it means "male (as stronger for lifting)."

In Strong's Concordance (#504 - Greek = *teknon*) is the word "child" and it means "a child (as produced) child, daughter, son."

The difference between the man and the child in this text is very clear. It makes absolutely no sense that the Rapture-harpazo of Rev 12:5 would include Jesus Christ (God **man**) in that He would be "caught up."

It's God Himself that performs the miracle of catching up and it is the born-again Christians (**child** church) that get caught up or Raptured.

What's also interesting about the words 'caught up"

(*harpazo*) in verse 5 is that it occurs just before verse 6 where the woman has *fled to the wilderness*. This is a sequence that exactly matches Paul's sequence in 1st Thessalonians.

Rev 12:6: "And the woman fled into the wilderness, where she hath a place prepared of God that they should feed her there a thousand two hundred and threescore days."

Does that number sound familiar? It should because it equals exactly three and a half years.

We now have three factors that help to clarify the location of the Rapture:

- The word "harpazo" in Revelation 12:5 is chronologically situated *after* the "great wonder" astronomical sign of Rev 12:1.

- The word "harpazo" in Revelation 12:5 is chronologically situated *before* the 1,260-day reference in Rev 12:6.

- Rev 12:6 is telling us that the woman (remnant of Israel) flees to the wilderness for exactly 1,260 days.

The woman is obviously fleeing to save her life from something or someone. She's in fact fleeing from the wrath of the newly revealed antichrist. This is the start of the three-and-a-half-year Great Tribulation.

Since there is no written time-span definition given for Rev 12 verses 1 through 4, it's impossible to pinpoint a start time. My theory that this was a good place to plug in Daniel's seventieth week would be valid *if* there was a direct reference made in the text to "seven times." It's just not there. Since there's no clear chronological reference available, to venture out on a limb with unsubstantiated chronology is not a good idea.

But there is another possible solution in God's use of a "sign" for signaling the onset of the most important seven-year period in all of human history, with a mid-point Rapture and a latter half-segment, Great Tribulation. Revelation 12 has at its very core an astronomical storyboard at work. What about looking for an indirect reference that makes use of the celestial realm?

The Disciples inquired of Jesus about end-time *signs*. His lengthy and detailed response was a confirmation that their sincere inquiry was justified.

The only sign that has a level of impact, divine provenance regarding Israel and is properly located in a section of prophetic scripture that describes a "Rapture" event and subsequent Great Tribulation, would be the one that the Apostle John describes in Revelation 12:1.

If any astronomical sign would be worthy of mention and placement in Luke 21:25, that would be the one. And that one was the "great wonder in heaven", which was the constellation Virgo crowned with Leo in its extremely rare twelve-star configuration. This sign event made its appearance on September 23, 2017.

The inclusion of *harpazo* (Rapture) within Revelation

12 allows for it to be useful in the locating/positioning of Daniel's seventieth week.

*

The concept of the Rapture is so incredible as to be almost unbelievable. To see the very specific and unique reference of *harpazo* appearing in two distinct places with a matching end-time context makes it more palpable to the person that is placing their hope in it.

This was accomplished perfectly by God in that the *harpazo* is found in Paul's letter to the Thessalonians and also in John's Book of Revelation.

14

The Rapture is Not The First Resurrection

The Second Coming of Jesus to planet Earth includes the following people:

- The saints of times past.
- The Raptured saints.
- The souls of saints that were killed during the Great Tribulation.

This section will hopefully clear up some misunderstanding about some (not all) post-Rapture events. The Rapture (*harpazo*) is a unique one-time event marked by a "catching away" or supernatural transporting and simultaneous transformation.

Although it can truly be said that the bodies of the "dead in Christ" are literally *resurrected,* the amazing Rapture/harpazo event is primarily and uniquely characterized in terms of its *sudden-extremely-fast-supernatural-evacuation-transformation-right-off-the-planet-Earth* nature.

This is clearly not the same event that is described as the "first resurrection" in Revelation 20:5 which is an event that is confined to the surface area of the planet. If it were a Rapture type event as is mentioned in Rev 12:5, then the Apostle John would simply have used the word *harpazo* again in Rev 20:5.

At the end of the Great Tribulation which is at the end of Daniel's seventieth week, all of the Raptured saints are making the return trip with Jesus Messiah back to planet Earth. They're all living in their permanent "Glorified" bodies as is Jesus Christ in His permanent "Glorified" body.

But there is another group of Christian people that are with them on the return trip. This group consists of the souls of the people who were saved (born again) and died during the Great Tribulation, who exist in their spiritual bodies only.

These people are not yet in their permanent glorified bodies. This is because during the Great Tribulation, their physical bodies were left dead on planet earth, which is typically what happens when anyone dies.

But for any Christian saint, to be absent from the body is to be present with the Lord. This stands true for all saints of the past, present and those who are on planet Earth during the Great Tribulation and are killed.

The soul moves on to be with God and the body is left behind. Remember, it's the soul that *is* the person.

These exact same Great Tribulation period Christian souls are identified earlier in Revelation 7:9-17.

Verse 9: "They are a 'great multitude' . . . of all nations . . ." Conclusion: This is a vast number of people from all over the world.

Verse 14: "These are they which came out of great tribulation . . ." Conclusion: God saved the souls of these people during the three-and-a-half-year Great Tribulation.

Verse 15: " . . . they are before the throne of God . . ." Conclusion: These saved "souls" are living in Heaven with God.

Rev 20:4 says " . . . and I saw the souls of them that were beheaded for the witness of Jesus, and for the word of God, and which had not worshipped the beast, neither his image, neither had received his mark upon their foreheads or in their hands; **and they lived and reigned with Christ a thousand years.**"

What John is saying here is that the "souls" of those killed in the Great Tribulation are eventually going to be living back on good ol' planet Earth with Jesus and this time period is going to be for one thousand years.

In order for this to happen, there would first have to be a resurrection taking place on planet Earth whereby their souls are reunited with their bodies in a permanent "Glorified" body state.

This would certainly have to be the case because there's no other way that they could physically live and reign for a thousand years. Their original old-type bodies would not last more than about seventy to 100 years.

Question: So what is it that awaits them (the Christians killed during the Great Tribulation) at the end of this trip back to planet Earth?

Answer: They will be re-united with their resurrected bodies in a "Glorified" body version in what is called the **"first resurrection."**

Question: What is the thousand-year long time period spoken of in Rev 20:4?

Answer: It is the thousand-year reign of Jesus Christ on Earth that closes out the 6th millennium.

Question: What does it mean in Mark 13:27 when Jesus said that He will "send His angels and gather his elect from the four winds, from the uttermost part of the earth to the uttermost part of heaven"?

Answer: When Jesus returns to planet Earth (Mark 13:26) at the conclusion of the Great Tribulation (Mark 13:24) He will dispatch his angels to gather *all* of His people. In many places in the scriptures, the children of God (born-again Christians) are referred to as the "elect."

Those "elect" in this particular instance will be:

- The living survivors of the Great Tribulation from all over the entire planet (the four winds / uttermost part of the earth = terrestrial).
- Those arriving with Jesus in the sky above (uttermost part of heaven = celestial).

This is a massive operation to gather Christians together from both realms. But because Jesus is actually *arriving physically to planet Earth* (Second Advent) with the full intention of *staying*, this mass gathering operation culminates on the terrestrial surface of planet Earth, not in the celestial heavens above.

In other words, this section (Rev 20:5) is *not* describing the Rapture.

15

Rapture Call Audio Characteristics

WITH A SHOUT,
WITH THE VOICE OF THE ARCHANGEL
AND WITH THE TRUMP OF GOD
—Paul to the Corinthians.

In 1st Corinthians 15:51-52, it basically says:

- Paul is revealing new information.
- There will be the avoidance of death and a transformation for the living Saints.
- The speed of the event is extremely fast.
- The audible sound of the trumpet (shofar) call is used and it's the very last trumpet blast that triggers the event.
- The dead bodies of saints past will be raised into a perfect new physical and spiritual state, as will the living saints.

Read verse 51: "Behold, I show you a mystery; we shall all

not sleep, but we shall all be changed."

Conclusion: The mystery is revealed. The living Saints will not die but be supernaturally transformed.

Read verse 52: "In a moment, in the twinkling of an eye, at the last trump: for the trumpet shall sound, and the dead shall be raised incorruptible, and we shall be changed."

Conclusion: The event happens suddenly and extremely fast. The very last blast of the trumpet is the one that actually turns the key. The bodies of dead Saints are raised and transformed into new, perfect, immortal beings and the living Saints are also raised (caught up) and transformed into the same kind of beings.

In 1st Thessalonians 4:15-17, it says:

- Paul is relaying information that he received directly from Jesus.
- There are two groups involved that are called and the order in which they are caught up is explained.
- The location of Jesus from which he makes the Rapture call is explained.
- There are three distinct types of notification used in succession.
- The atmospheric location of the place-of-gathering/meeting is explained.
- There is a statement that says from that point onward we are going to be with the Lord.

Read verse 15: "For this we say unto you by the word of the Lord, that we which are alive and remain unto the coming of the Lord shall not precede them which are asleep."

Conclusion: Paul received this information first hand from Jesus (The Lord) himself. The living Saints will not be Raptured prior to the dead Saints bodies being raised up, but immediately after they are raised up.

Read verse 16: "For the Lord himself will descend from heaven with a shout, with the voice of the archangel, and with the trump of God; and the dead in Christ shall rise first."

Conclusion: "Jesus, who is now stationed in the upper atmosphere of planet Earth, is going to direct his attention downward toward his people on earth. His voice is unmistakable in its unique characteristic power and majesty. An archangel announces immediately after that. There is finally the accompaniment of the blowing of a trumpet for an undetermined number of blasts. The dead bodies of Saints past are raised up to the upper atmosphere where Jesus is stationed and supernaturally reunited (reassembled) with their owners, who have previously existed in a spiritual form in heaven with God.

Read verse 17: "Then we which are alive and remain shall be caught up together with them in the clouds, to meet the Lord in the air: and so shall we ever be with the Lord."

Conclusion: The Saints who are alive are then caught up (after the dead in Christ), supernaturally transformed and are also in the same upper atmospheric level (station) with Jesus. This newly gathered group would from that time forward be living in a new realm or "kingdom" that is presided over by God himself.

The Rapture event is miraculous beyond anything imaginable. For God to resurrect the bodies of dead Saints from wherever they're located beneath the ground off of every continent would be an amazing thing. But does an all-powerful God need to open boxes in order to remove the contents?

What if their decomposed remains exist only in very tiny microscopic particles scattered all over the planet? I don't think that will be any problem for God whatsoever. He can create matter, so He can certainly reassemble matter.

When you add the living saints from planet Earth to that group, you've got a really huge amount of people. These two groups are then gathered way up above the Earth and have been fully transformed into new bodies that are built to last an eternity.

As Paul so nicely states this mystery in 1st Cor 15:54: "this corruptible shall have put on incorruption, and this mortal shall have put on immortality."

The speed is explained by the Apostle Paul as "in a moment, in the twinkling of an eye." That's an extremely brief moment—a split second, that's all. But God really doesn't need any more than that.

The audible annunciation made just before the Rapture consists of the vocal *shout* from Jesus, a voice from an anonymous archangel and then comes the trumpet blasts.

When Paul uses the phrase "at the last trump" (1st Cor 15:52) he is saying that there is more than one single trumpet blast. It's actually a set of trumpet blasts.

Exactly how many, we're not exactly sure. But Paul makes it clear that there is indeed a *last trumpet blast*.

Now I'm going list out some normal human reactions that would happen in response to a sudden announcement that could come at them from out of the clear blue. Remember, all of us at some time have been jolted by an unexpected crash or boom sound and our adrenaline was instantly kicked up several notches. It is assumed here that this is the literal Rapture call and each Christian hears it, whether they expect it or not.

- The initial element of shock or surprise.
- The realization that the sound is supernatural.
- The recovery of mental focus and concentration.

I think that God is fully aware of the effects that the Rapture call would have on His people and would graciously give a brief amount of "buffer" time for them to settle down after the initial surprise.

I'm guessing that the entire end-to-end annunciation will be at least twenty seconds in length, or maybe up to a full minute.

I also believe that Paul is describing a very special audio progression that God has designed for his people that will override any immediate distractions.

Christians of every country would naturally be hearing this call in their own language. In real-life experience it could work in this way.

Step 1: The vocal shout from Jesus is given first and is meant to grab our attention. The sound is like nothing else that we've ever heard for its power, clarity, focus and supernatural quality.

Step 2: Immediately after that is the voice of the archangel. Exactly what he says is unknown but a good guess might be "(your name here) come up hither" or "come up here." At this point we should be absolutely 100% tuned-in and very intent on listening further.

The "progression" from vocal to trumpet is the key.

Step 3: Then the trumpet blasts start to annunciate. They are heard, recognized and the progression is understood. We who have been called and are listening now have an actual audio confirmation that this is the Rapture call. We know for sure that *this is the moment.*

Step 4: A heightened state of spiritual anticipation would kick in as the attention is brought into alignment with the cadence of the trumpet annunciation. The trumpet blasts would continue until finished ("last trump") and the miracle called the Rapture finally happens: caught up = *harpazo* = presto gone!

Again, this subject is very difficult to fully explain and should be clearly understood as a "one-time-never-anything-like-it-before" type of miracle.

The fact that Paul would go to such great length in detailing this important annunciation shows that the Rapture itself is to be taken very seriously.

The fact of a specific "format" to the annunciation is also important to understand because it has a progressive "crescendo" feature that is not accidental.

The extreme nature of divine annunciation and subsequent evacuation also serves to qualify this entire event as a prophetic sign to the remaining population. The concept of a "called out" people finds literal meaning and proper placement at the mid-point of the timeline chart.

16

Do You See What I See?

Imagine a little orbital path and conjunction experiment in your own back yard.

Place a three-foot diameter beach ball on the lawn. This will represent the sun.

Take a small pebble (planet Earth) sized at one half inch in diameter in your one hand and a small pinch of sand to carry in your other hand. Stand back about eight feet away from the beach ball.

Have a friend take another pebble (planet Exit) sized at one-inch diameter and have them stand around thirty feet away from the beach ball.

This beach ball and pebble scenario is actually somewhat accurate in terms of comparative planetary body sizes.

One caveat though: please remember that although this experiment has all the action happening at ground level (single level orbital plane), the reality of this scenario is that in outer space, the orbital planes (not plane as in "airplane," but as in a path of travel) would probably not be exactly the same. They could be offset by many degrees.

OK, let's start the planets into motion.

You begin moving in a quick steady circular pattern around the sun with your pebble and maintain a distance of eight feet. You're duplicating the orbital path of the Earth around the sun.

Now have your friend walk very slowly towards the sun (first approach) in a gently curving path that targets an approximate ten-foot distance perimeter from the sun.

Remember, the path that your friend is taking is actually a long "elliptical" path, not a perfect circle.

At some point around the ten-to-twelve-foot perimeter from the sun your paths will converge and you'll be in fairly close proximity to each other. Be careful not to get too close at this juncture because we don't want the two planets to collide!

When you and your friend are both in very close proximity (place of intersection), take your pinch of sand and dump it into the free hand of your friend.

Your friend now has the pinch of sand in their hand.

You are moving onward on your regular circular orbit.

Your friend continues onward and needs to start taking a circular path of nine to ten feet from the sun and maintaining it until they have completed a total of 180 degrees of travel around the sun.

Your friend also needs to maintain this critical nine to ten foot safety distance because we wouldn't want them to get burnt up by the heat thrown off by the sun!

After completing their circular trip around the sun, your friend starts to straighten out and falls back into the elliptical path.

Your friend (with Planet Exit and the sand) is now heading back (second approach) in the direction they originally came from.

You are still walking around the eight-foot circular pattern at the same brisk pace.

At the same distance of around eight to ten feet from the sun, you and your friend will meet again at a fairly close "place of intersection." At this critical junction point, your friend reaches out and puts the pinch of sand back into your free hand.

Your friend continues to move away on their elliptical path. You continue on your circular path around the sun.

What just happened?

Phase 1) The important cargo was transferred from planet Earth to planet Exit on its elliptical orbit "ingress" path. This represents the "caught up" or Rapture event.

Phase 2) The important cargo was transferred from planet Exit back to planet Earth on the elliptical orbit "egress" path. This represents the Second Advent event.

Do you see that? Regarding the orbital chronology:

- The Phase 1 elliptical ingress segment would last 1 year and 9 months.
- The Phase 2 elliptical egress segment would last 1 year and 9 months.

Could such a basic orbital scenario involving planets be the actual designated method of God for the Rapture (*har-*

pazo) and the Second Advent? I don't know for sure, but here's something quite interesting found in Revelation.

Revelation 21:1 says "And I saw a new heaven and a new earth." I'm going to focus on the latter part of the sentence, "new earth."

Strong's concordance (Ref #1093) defines the word earth as soil, globe, earth, and world and is also inclusive of its "occupants." Sure sounds like a new planet to me.

It's well-known that this entire solar system works with gravitational fields that determine orbital paths of planets and the system works just fine.

On a much smaller scale, the tiny atom is an orbital system and it also works just fine. All this is not a fluke. It's clearly divine design.

Astrophysics does not negate or circumvent the prophetic future. I would strongly suggest that astrophysics supports it.

Diagram representing the suggested astronomy in Chapter 16

Note: This diagram (not to perfect scale) acknowledges that the Earth takes one day to orbit the sun and that Planet Exit would be moving at a much slower speed on a much longer extended elliptical path, totally independent of the Earth's standard orbital cycle. However, given the physics of orbital cycles, a close-proximity conjunction of the two planets is still possible.

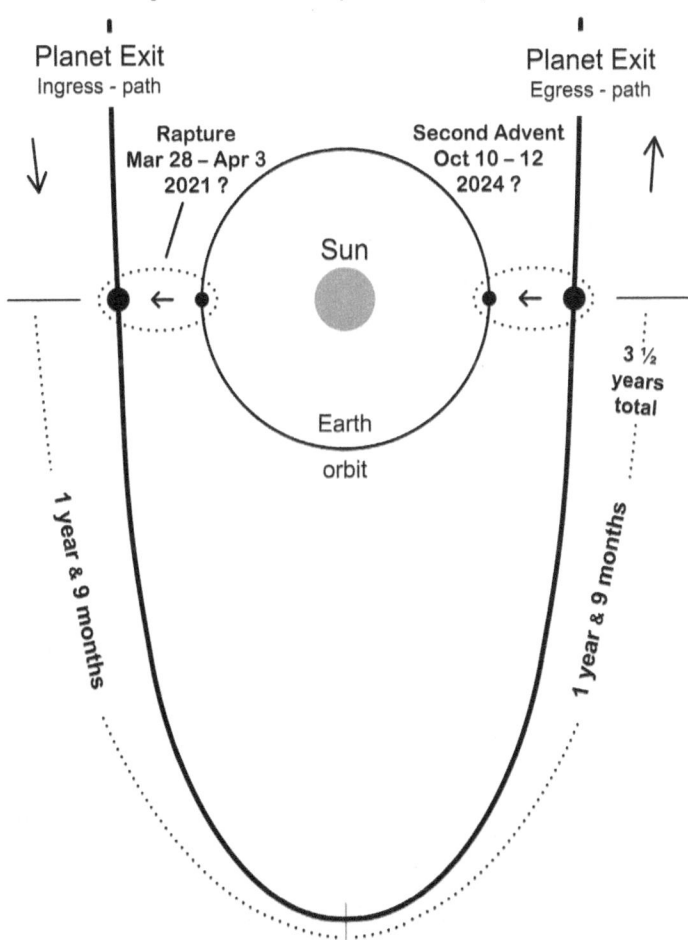

17

Guidelines for the Timeline Chart

The timeline chart for Daniel's seventieth week only took a few weeks to put together but about ten years or more for accumulating all the data necessary for it.

Daniel's first two linked segments (7 weeks and 62 weeks) offer a glimpse into God's timing methodology. The two segments are precisely measured timeframes with definite stated future events tied to them. That's fine.

But the big problem with the third 1-week segment is that it's not directly chronologically linked to the 62-week segment. There's an unknown time-span gap between segment #2 and segment #3. The playbook seems to missing some details that would help to locate the start time.

So I was faced with the prospect of having to research a lot of loose information that needed to combine properly before the picture could become clear.

The main thing for me was realizing that God's planning is "long range" planning.

This became apparent to me when I understood the structure of Daniel's seventy weeks. This meant that I had to lock into this concept and work with it.

God has a plan that he's developed and the clock is ticking away. But how and when does the finish line come into view?

The other thing was that God's celestial system is a divine clockwork system. It's a complimentary visual method that works in conjunction with linear time.

But the celestial realm is a bit tricky. There's a tremendous amount of activity in the cosmos and it needs to be filtered accordingly. The astro-prophetic puzzle pieces should all snap properly into place and the picture has to make sense.

My best option was to look for astronomical sign type event that could provide a point of reference. Once I settled into the Revelation 12:1 sign as the best option, the puzzle pieces began to fall into place.

The basic heavenly Virgo-Leo combo sign, a *Leo* constellation appearing in its normal "nine-star" configuration, was indeed demonstrated by Rick Larson to have direct bearing on the First Advent. This is an absolute fact.

To me, it would make sense that this unique celestial display should reappear for the Second Advent, but it should reappear in a configuration that *perfectly matches* the details given by the Apostle John in Rev 12:1. That perfect match would be the Leo "twelve-star" crown configuration.

To start the guideline assembly process, I'll cover the long-range chronology first and use major event "markers" at important intervals. This is actually how I personally organized it after I had filtered out the non-essential data and condensed the material that was absolutely necessary to complete the picture.

For me, the idea of long-range planning means that establishing valid Biblical historical chronology had to be done before anything else. The basis for my timeline chart must have its accuracy supported with accurate Biblical records if it's going to be useful.

After that, I'll incorporate the key elements of astronomy and God's divine feast schedule to provide more detail.

What the heck, I'll even throw in some lucky number sevens for good measure!

Let's first take a look at the long-term Biblical calendar for some data that references standard historical time frames and see if some very important markers will appear.

Let's start with a broad-overview template that has a Biblical history of 6000 years and divide it into three 2000-year segments:

- Adam to Abraham is 2000 years. 2000 years is the elapsed time-span and Abraham is the significant marker of interest.

- Abraham to Jesus Christ first Advent is 2000 years. 2000 years is the time span and Jesus Christ is the significant marker of interest.

- Jesus Christ first Advent to now is 2000-plus years. 2000 years is the time span and we're still waiting.

All totaled it basically equals 6000-plus years and there's supposed to be some fireworks happening about now.

Now let's overlay this broad-overview template with the historically based long-range Jubilee (50-year) cycle template and see where the important markers appear.

I'm going to stay with a very basic overview here because to list out all the events throughout history that correspond to the 50- and 100-year marks would be enough for another book altogether.

According to Jewish Hebrew scholars, the total number of Jubilee cycles for this same broad-overview world history time span is 120. The teaching basically says that there are 120 Jubilee cycles (6000 years) from the time God created the earth until the beginning of the prophesied Messianic Kingdom. The group of 120 is typically broken into two segments of 50 and 70 Jubilees.

- From Creation to Exodus there are 50 Jubilees making 2500 years.
- From Exodus (1483 B.C.) to 2017 there are seventy Jubilees making 3500 years.

2500 plus 3500 equals 6000 years . . . easy math. So both templates match up and that makes for a confirmation of the broad overview.

The Jubilee long-range span and the 6 millennia timespan would all be concluded right about now if in fact all of their start times were actually the same.

Seeing as we're talking about time-spans in light of "Biblical" history, I'm going to use a synchronized starting point of about 3983 BC.

This starting point of 3983 BC was derived by the late John Ogwyn in his 6-segment count from year 0 back to Adam. This system is 100% accurate because it only uses the reference points (timeline markers) in the Old Testament that consist of verifiable dates and time spans involving known people and real events.

This is what I believe to be the most reliable method for calculating a true historical Biblical chronology.

The 6 segments of time measurement are as follows:

Segment 1
From: Year 0.
Back to: The 4th year of Solomon's reign (secular historical documentation) when the temple construction (1st Kings 6:1) was started.
Time: 966 years.

Segment 2
From: Solomon 4th year / temple construction.
Back to: The Exodus (Exodus 12:40).
Time: 480 years.

Segment 3
From: The Exodus.

Back to: Abrahamic covenant (Gal 3:16-17).
Time: 430 years.

Segment 4
From: Abrahamic covenant.
Back to: Abraham at time of Circumcision covenant at Haran and the death of Terah. (Gen 17:1-10)
Time: 24 years.

Segment 5
From: Abraham at time of Circumcision covenant at Haran and the death of Terah.
Back to: The Flood (Gen 11:1-10).
Time: 427 years.

Segment 6
From: The Flood.
Back to: Creation of Adam (Gen 5:3-29) - Add the ages of patriarchs plus Noah.
Time: 1,656 years.

Total
1,656 + 427 + 24 + 430 + 480 + 966 = **3,983 years.**

This is the "BC" chronology that reflects truly accurate Biblical history.

There's another resource that supports this more recent

starting point of creation that was considered to be of the very finest scholarship and thorough research.

In the 1650s, James Usher published "Annals of the World" in which he stated the beginning of the world took place on Oct 23 4004 BC (Julian). The 4004 BC date is generally acceptable for a Biblically based long-range 6000-year Earth history. I'm staying with Johns Ogwyn's calculation.[3]

There's one other thing I want to throw in at this point in the study. If you ever encounter someone who wants to argue in favor of a multi-billion-year evolutionary time frame, just be polite and hang up the phone.

Here's a 6 millennium breakdown using the 3983 BC start date:

> Year 3983 BC* to 2983 BC = 1 Millennium
> Year 2983 BC to 1983 BC = 1 millennium
> Year 1983 BC to 0983 BC = 1 millennium
> Year 0983 BC to 0017 AD = 1 millennium
> Year 0017 BC to 1017 AD = 1 millennium
> Year 1017 AD to 2017 AD = 1 millennium

> *(or starting point of year 0)*

Add them all up you get a total of 6000 years. It's a fact that this is now year 2019 and the 6000 years are well behind

---

3   Detailed information on the 3,983 calculation can be found at: www.cogwriter.com/six_thousand_year_plan_6000.htm

us. But don't pack up and head to the nearest mountaintop just quite yet. There's more.

Remember back in Chapter 5 where Julius Caesar implemented his Julian calendar and later Gregory modified it? Well folks, they pulled a fast one on us. Their calendar system does indeed function for the world, but it doesn't provide for perfect "prophetic biblical" sync.

I'm going to sidestep around Greg's "prophetic" sync error and look for some different information that could reveal the Biblically based location for the beginning of Daniel's seventieth week. This means the timing information that I want has absolutely nothing to do with the Gregorian calendar system.

September 20-21 of 2017 officially closes out the Hebrew calendar year of 5776-5777. It's this same 5777 that is understood by many Hebrew scholars to be the conclusion of the 6th millennium.

The year 5776-5777 is also a Jubilee year that marks the end of a Jubilee (fifty-year-long) cycle.

September 21-22 (Rosh Hashanah) brings in the 5777-5778 New Year.

According to traditional Hebrew understanding, beyond this 5776-5777 barrier is a very important *prophetic* period that is understood as the 7th millennium. This key 7th millennium is supposed to be one in which the return of the Messiah happens. His role as King of Kings to reign over His eternal kingdom is assumed to happen sometime at the beginning of this period.

For a good candidate to signal the start Daniel's seventieth week, we need the following:

- A strong end-times prophetic "sign" emphasis.
- A location at the end of the 6000-year time span as detailed in this chapter.
- A definite mention in the Book of Revelation.
- An association with a pre-3½ year Great Tribulation.

The "Great Wonder" sign of Revelation 12:1 that appeared on September 23, 2017 is the best candidate. It meets all the above listed criteria and it also had an actual chronologically proximate placement that marked the crossing of the 5777 barrier.

It just so happens that in this event there is also a significant relationship to the number seven. It's obvious that the Biblical legacy year of 5777 has *three sevens* in the time stamp. This follows my theory (see Chapter 6) that there is a message conveyance factor involved in the repetition of the number seven.

Now let's consider the celestial storyboard. Remember, this system intentionally incorporates both a character based narrative and an astronomically based narrative to make the point.

Question: Why is it that the constellation Leo (the Lion / Judah = the Royal line among the twelve tribes of Israel) just happens to show up in its ultra-rare twelve-star "crown" configuration over the head of Virgo (Israel) immediately after the year of 5777 is completed?

Answer: It's very possible that at some point in time not long after 5777 there is going to be a Royal "coronation." In other words, 5777 might have signaled ahead to the station to let them know the train is carrying a very important person of Royal stature and is soon to arrive.

Recall back in Chapter 4 where the word "moad" translates to "appointments" as indicated by the celestial? This Leo-twelve-star-crown event has all the earmarks of a divine appointment that has been strategically situated in the celestial storyboard.

But seeing as this event is so vitally important, wouldn't God give some additional confirmation? Is there anything of a cyclical schedule-based nature that could support this as a proposed start date? Are there any longer-range markers that can be plugged in?

If you add 3½ years to the Rev 12:1 sign of 9-23-17, you arrive at Passover of 2021, March 28 to April 3rd. This is noteworthy because of its location at the halfway point of the 7-year span where one would hope to find a "Passover/Exodus/Rapture" type event.

Now let's take a look at the latter 3½-year period (second half segment) that immediately follows Passover of 2021. This time period segment would run from early April of 2021 to early October of 2024. The timeline chart identifies this segment as the Great Tribulation.

Are there any significant celestial events noted in

prophesy that fall within this latter 3-1/2-year period and thereby serve as timeline markers?

Yes there are. Joel 2:31 says, "The sun shall be turned into darkness, and the moon into blood, before the great and terrible day of the Lord come."

The turning of the "sun into darkness" would imply a total solar eclipse. The turning of the "moon into blood" would imply a "total lunar eclipse" or blood moon.

Is there the appearance of these two celestial sign events appearing somewhere within the latter 3½-year period (after April 2021) and are they appearing in the exact same order (sequence) that Joel indicated? (In other words, a total solar eclipse *must appear first* and a total lunar eclipse *must appear second.*)

Yes there is. On December 4th of 2021 there will be a total solar eclipse and on May 15th of 2022 there will be a total lunar eclipse. We have a match.

Let's move on to the end of the latter 3½-year segment and see what shows up. That brings the timeline to October of 2024 and hopefully we'll find some important events there. There's a couple celestial events detailed in scripture as an ominous precursor to the return of Jesus Christ to planet Earth.

Jesus said: (the first part of Matthew 24:29) "Immediately after the tribulation of those days shall the sun be darkened, and the moon shall not give her light . . ."

The text here in Matthew is clearly indicating a *reduction in luminescent output,* not a total blackout as in a total eclipse. Let's check out the similar end-times prophesies of Joel 3:15 and Isaiah 13:10.

- Joel 3:15 says, "The sun and the moon shall be darkened..."
- Isaiah 13:10 says "... the sun shall be darkened in his going forth and the moon shall not cause her light to shine."

The texts here in Joel and Isaiah clearly indicate a *reduction in luminescent output,* not a total blackout as in a total eclipse.

If the timeline chart has the potential to be correct, then there should definitely be the appearance of two celestial events of this nature located at the very end, sometime in October of 2024.

On October 2nd of 2024 there is an annular solar eclipse scheduled to happen and it's pretty obvious that the sun will be darkened. On October 2nd of 2024 there is a new moon scheduled to happen and it's pretty obvious that the moon will not give her light.

The prophetic texts of Matthew 24:29, Joel 3:15 and Isaiah 13:10 all synchronize perfectly at this juncture. We have a match.

The latter part of Matthew 24:29 says "... and the stars shall fall from heaven, and the powers of the heavens shall be shaken."

This is a very difficult section to interpret because there are no previous astronomical events that bear any resemblance to the "falling stars" and "shaking powers" that are mentioned here. It's a totally new thing and cannot be officially charted. However, I thought it was important enough to include as additional information only.

The storyboard, in my opinion, would feature some astronomical phenomenon that brings attention to the bright Glory of God for His return. The idea for using the celestial realm for the purpose of divine emphasis in this situation makes perfect sense. Planet Earth will not be able to optically deny what is about to happen.

Let's examine the word "shaken." Strong's concordance (#4531) defines this as "to waver, rock and topple." This has the idea of intentional forcible disruption by God himself.

The entire verse 29 also needs to be analyzed from end-to-end in order to understand the meaning in terms of a basic technical overview.

Some people like to take this verse and spin it with various allegorical inventions. They can't seem to accept that God owns the celestial. It's totally His domain and He controls the lights, the wiring and the power plant. So the divine ownership factor should make it clear to anyone that the heavenly reference of verse 29 must mean that the context is astronomy, plain and simple.

In the totality of verse 29, the celestial lights (greater being the sun and lesser being the moon) that illuminate the planet Earth and additionally the bright spots in the surrounding universe (stars), are being dimmed out and removed from view.

Why would that be? All the heavenly light sources that can normally be seen from planet Earth are being turned off by God in order to allow for the unmistakable brightness and glory of Jesus Christ to be seen by observers on planet Earth.

- Matthew 24:30 says "and then shall appear the sign of the Son of man in heaven."
- 2nd Thessalonians 2:8 says " . . . with the brightness of his coming."

How are we able to see the planets out in outer space? We're able to see them because of the light reflected off the surface area that is facing towards the planet Earth.

If all the lights in the heavens are switched off, how would we (on Earth) be able to see anything that is headed towards our planet?

Rev 21:23 says "And the city had no need of the sun, neither the moon, to shine in it: for the glory of God did lighten it, and the Lamb is the light thereof."

Here's another example of extremely high light emission generated by divinity.

Matthew 17:2 gives the account of the transfiguration: "And was transfigured before them; and his face did shine as the sun, and his raiment was white as the light."

These two verses describe luminescent output in terms of wide-angle dispersion and single source point. Both are being attributed to divinity, God.

This lone (self-illuminated) object (Planet Exit) would

be in approach to the planet Earth and could qualify as the "sign" of His Second Coming. The source of the extremely high light emission here would have to be divinity in none other than the person of Jesus Christ Himself.

Back to timeline markers. Is there a subsequent cyclical schedule-based event that would support a narrative suggesting salvation, rescue or restoration?

Yes there is. There's a scheduled event that relates directly to Jesus the Messiah because He atoned for our sins in order to bring us to Him. Yom Kippur (Day of Atonement) is on October 12, 2024.

Throughout scripture it's evident the God wants to fellowship with mankind. Is there an event following the Day of Atonement that speaks to this idea? Yes there is. The Feast of Tabernacles is on October 17-23.

The seventieth week timeline chart has a storyline integrated into it that you can't miss. It's so well coordinated that it could only have been designed by divinity.

Additionally, this particular 7-year timeline seems to carry enough apocalyptic punch to make it a very good candidate for "Daniel's seventieth Week."

To sum it all up: the data in this book *suggests a possible* end-time framework (using current familiar Gregorian calendar system) with the following:

Daniel's seventieth week began on 9-23-17 signaled by the great wonder in heaven sign of Revelation 12:1.

Add 3½ years.

The Rapture occurs in early April of 2021 during the

Feast of Passover (a seven-day period from March 28 to April 3) and most likely at the end of the feast.

Add 3½ years of Great Tribulation.

The Second Advent of Jesus Christ Messiah (the Day of the Lord) could happen sometime in early to mid October 2024. The following pages display a sequence of graphic images to illustrate this information in the form of a timeline chart.

Celestial Activity Prior to Rev 12:1

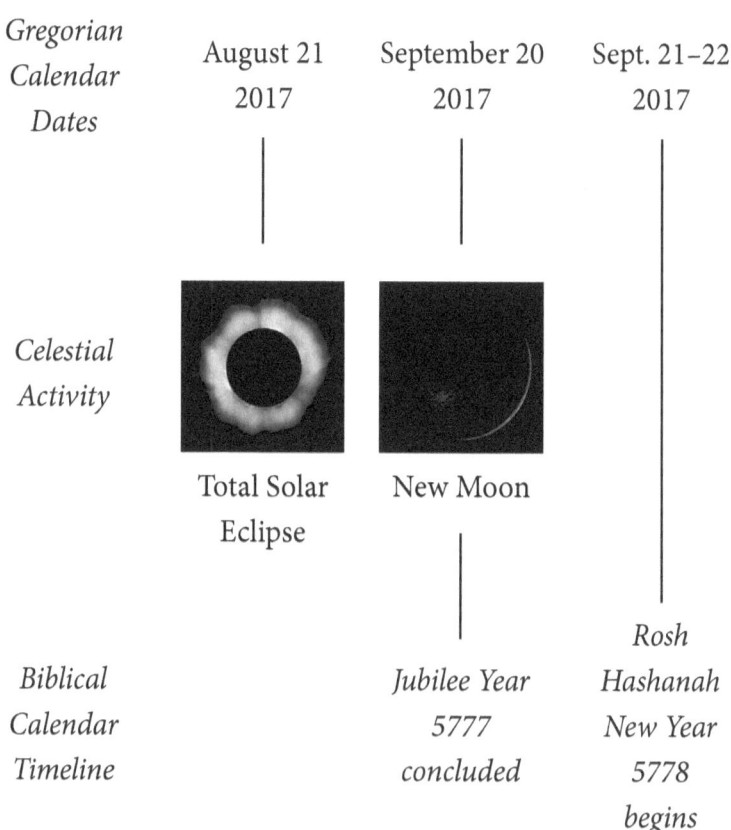

Celestial Activity After Rev 12:1

Daniel's 70th Week: First Half

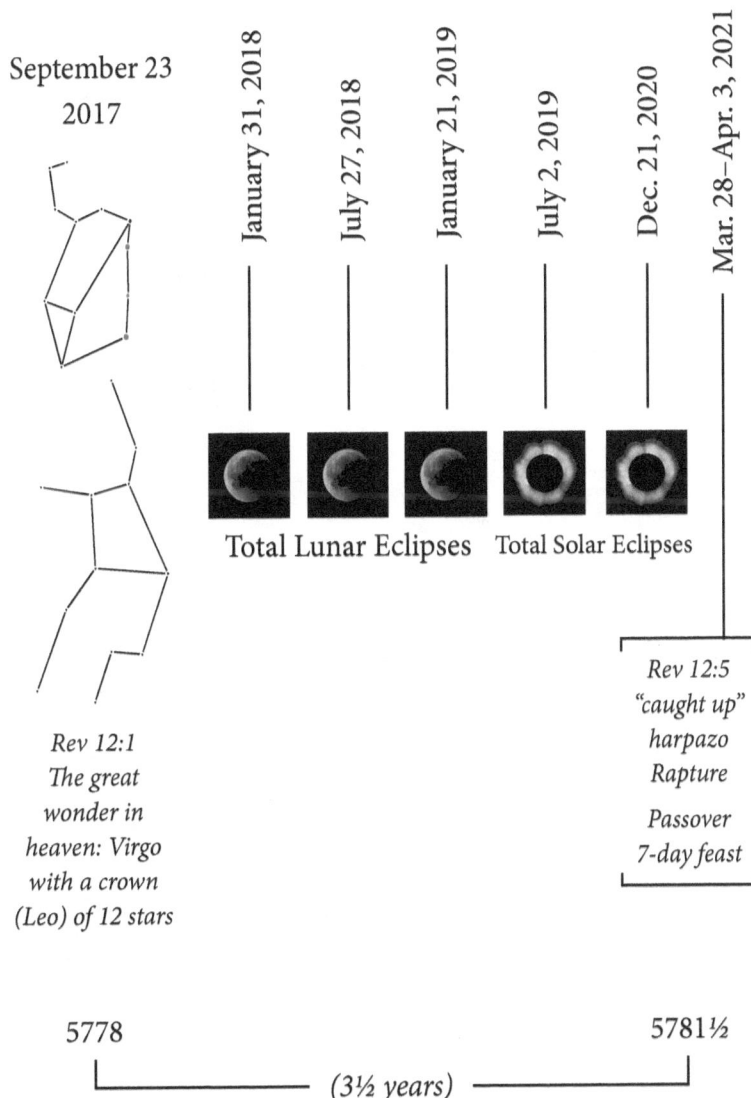

September 23 2017

January 31, 2018
July 27, 2018
January 21, 2019
July 2, 2019
Dec. 21, 2020
Mar. 28–Apr. 3, 2021

Total Lunar Eclipses   Total Solar Eclipses

Rev 12:1
The great wonder in heaven: Virgo with a crown (Leo) of 12 stars

Rev 12:5
"caught up" harpazo Rapture

Passover 7-day feast

5778   5781½

⎯⎯⎯ (3½ years) ⎯⎯⎯

Daniel's 70th Week: Second Half / Great Tribulation

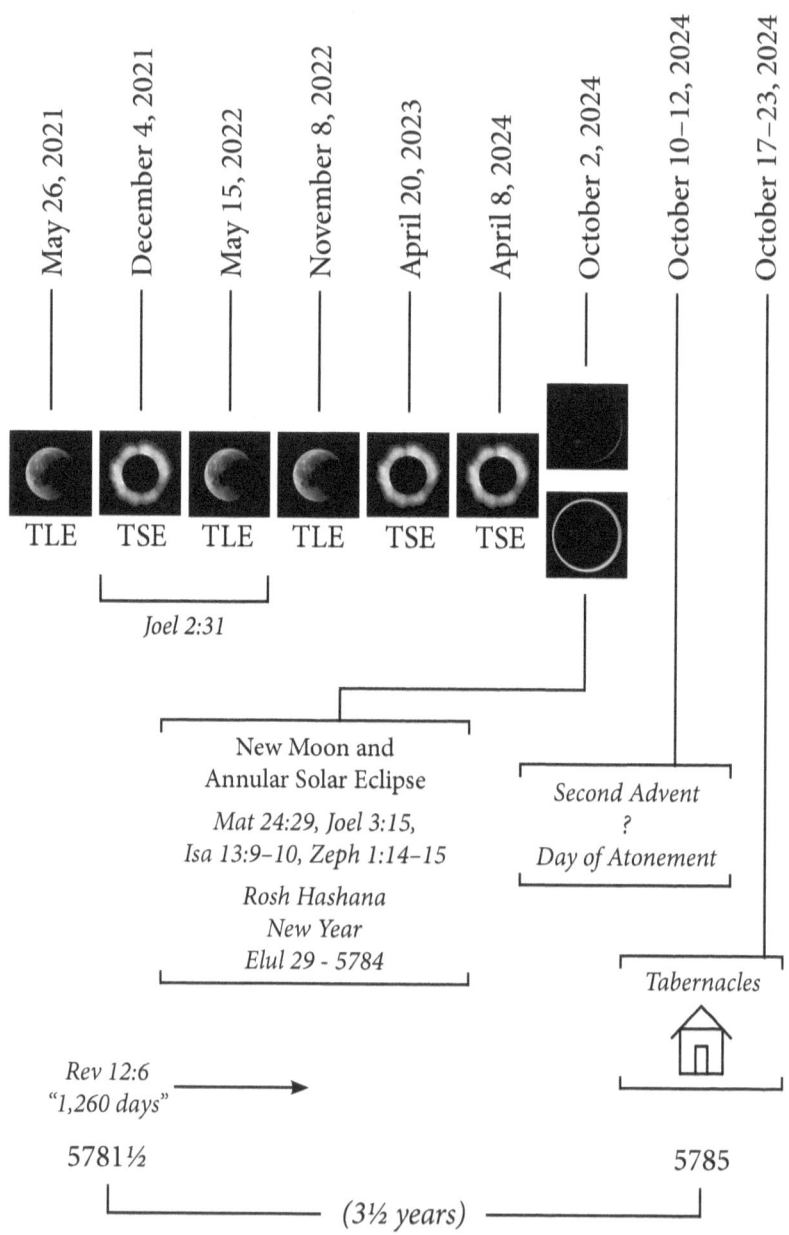

18

THE FUTURE BEYOND THE SECOND ADVENT

So far, this book has examined the chronology leading up to and ending with the time of just beyond the 6000-year (5777) threshold. Right after that, this time span culminates with the Second Advent of Christ Messiah.

There has been a lot of information presented and it will probably take some time to let it all sink in. I would suggest that in the course of considering this information, you would not be opposed to doing a little stargazing or web surfing on the subject of recent discoveries in the celestial realm.

Hopefully, the main idea of a divine chronological template that's in play will be the thing that you can take away from this book.

If you look closely at the very end of the timeline chart, there is a little house or "booth." This is indicating the start of the millennial reign on Earth, which is kicked off with the Feast of Tabernacles. This time is traditionally celebrated by the participants having to live in booths (huts) during the entire seven days of this festival.

But what's with the booths? They are symbolic of the fact that God desires for His people to celebrate a communion with him in a setting that He has predetermined. The accommodations are admittedly rather humble but there's nothing really wrong with that.

Rustic accommodations aside, this is supposed to be a time when the debris of tribulation have passed away, the dust has settled and there is perfect peace and tranquility. This is a time when the Creator will enjoy being with his creation.

And of course, as this celebration is indeed an actual feast, there will no doubt be food served. And I'm guessing that the food will be nothing less than excellent. Whether or not there will be booth service I really don't know. But having to walk a little way to a regular buffet style setup is OK with me. I always was curious about manna so maybe some of that will be available too.

Bonus: All the food on planet Earth from this time forward will be *non-GMO!* You've got to love that, right?! No more MSG, artificial preservatives, yellow dye, red dye, partially hydrogenated oils, diglycerides, toxicisides (I made that up), nitrates, glyphosates, artificial sweeteners or any other unhealthy additives.

Now for the *big one*: will there be chocolate? I'm not sure. I hope so.

And because God has ordained this special "Tabernacles-Fellowship" occasion as a yearly event, it will be held every year and run for the entire length of the millennial reign, which is 1,000 years.

The traditional understanding of the Genesis creative period works like this: God created the world and everything in it in six days and then he rested on the seventh day.

In regard to its long-range parallel in a millennial sense, after the 6th millennium is finished, the 7th millennium of rest or eternity begins.

And what do the scriptures say about this point in time with regards to astronomy? As covered back in Chapter 15, Revelation 21:1 says "And I saw a new heaven and a new earth." From what I can ascertain from this verse, the new heaven and new earth definitely mean a major move for God's people.

But what's the actual implication here? I think it would be this: a literal mass transfer of the old Earth's entire population to a new planet (new Earth) as mentioned in the verse.

What about the "new heaven"? I personally believe that what it's referring to is a new solar system. The two (planets and solar system) would go hand in hand so I don't see any point in entertaining a different scenario. In postulating this theory, I'm not venturing into abstract or absurd conceptual ground. My opinion is that the existing model of our solar system is a good working model.

What's more, I believe that what was also revealed to the Apostle John in the Revelation, if he didn't already know it, was the fact of our planet being part of a system containing other planetary bodies.

There's another thing that I came to understand about God's long-range planning. There is a very clear intent on His part to assign the proprietorship of his real estate to His people.

Take the example of Adam and Eve. God placed them in the garden to tend and keep it. But also told them to create more human beings in order to populate the entire planet.

Genesis 1:28 is very clear: "And God said to them, Be fruitful, and multiply, and replenish the earth, and subdue it: and have dominion over the fish of the sea, and over the fowl of the air, and over every living thing that moveth upon the earth."

This initiative was well supported by a home base, the Garden of Eden that had a wonderful supply of provisions. You must have adequate provisions in order to expand the operation and that's exactly what God had set up for them.

Unfortunately, as the story goes, this plan was sidetracked by the fall of Adam and Eve. They were tossed out of their beautiful dwelling place and things have only got worse since then.

Genesis 9:1: After taking Noah and his family on a long boat ride to the mountains of Ararat, he told them these familiar words: "Be fruitful, and multiply, and replenish the earth."

Here's yet another example. Abraham and the covenant people who were to dwell in the land that God had given to them. In later years, under the leadership of Joshua, this people group eventually made it into to the land that God designated for them. It was a land of milk and honey. Provisions were plentiful.

Gen 12:1: "Now the Lord had said to Abram, Get thee out of thy country, and from thy kindred, and from thy father's house, unto a land that I will shew thee:

Gen 12:2: "And I will make of thee a great nation, and I will bless thee, and make thy name great; and thou shall be a blessing..."

But again, as the story goes, eventually they took things for granted, became lazy and proud, crossed a line that they were not supposed to cross and were subsequently displaced from their nice dwelling place.

Sounds like a broken record doesn't it? Well, even though the record is broken, the record player still works fine. There's still a faithful God in authority that stands firm on His original initiative and it's going to happen. And it will happen according to His schedule.

Let's look at Revelation 21:1 for some more astronomy. It says "And I saw a new heaven and a new earth."

It looks like after the 6th millennium has concluded, God will have a new dwelling place already prepared. And just why would He go to all the trouble of preparing this new dwelling place? It's because He has a long-range plan to have fellowship with His created beings.

Going forward from the time of the completion of the 6th millennium is eternity. I'm sure that none of us can comprehend such a long, drawn out future. I sometimes wonder about it, but I really can't fully grasp it. Wouldn't we all get bored playing our harps after just a couple of weeks? ☹

Seriously though, God made us in His image and that means we were designed to be healthy in mind, spirit, and body—active, and doing productive things.

As far as the productivity part goes, I believe that God likes productivity. It's a blessing to be able to imagine, design, calculate, build, and then see whatever it is that you've built actually function.

There are so many wonderful things to learn about. I believe that God likes for His people to be interested in studying His creation.

I'm also convinced that an infinite God has the ability to plan for eternity. And if that plan hails back to His original initiative, then it's clear that He intends for His people to continue to increase in number.

And if that statement is true, then it stands to reason that this type of expansion would require more real estate.

It just so happens that God designed a universe that is "expanding." But if the universe is expanding, what is it expanding into?

It's expanding into His vacant celestial property. I can't say for certain, but I'll bet that He has plans to develop it. ☺

Sound interesting?

In Closing

Within the segment of the population that concerns itself with the Second Advent, there have been way too many knee-jerk reactions.

A person or a group will identify a certain astronomical event that has prophetic implications and then reach a conclusion about it. Then they'll make a plan in response to it. So far, these plans have always ended up in fizzle city.

Here's a tech-sector analogy that I've drawn from my own personal experience. It may help to explain what's been going on with all the knee-jerk reactions that have taken place over the last hundred years or so.

In the telecom world we have devices called routers. These are the machines that move data traffic around the networks, including the World Wide Web.

These machines can diagnose their own problems and produce a record (error log) for the engineers to use in troubleshooting.

Let's say that over several days, a certain router has been having problems and the error log is showing multiple intermittent circuit card failures.

The log shows the errors (signs) in order of severity.

So they replace the questionable single circuit cards beginning from the highest severity to the lowest severity.

Then the error log is re-checked.

But the errors are still showing up!

Kicking the thing won't help.

A senior engineer takes over and finds an older error that indicates the *motherboard*, which all the circuit cards plug into, is going bad.

Finally the motherboard is replaced, the router comes back up and all the errors clear. In retrospect, reactionary knee-jerk (single circuit card) plans have not been working. So in prophetic terms, what does the motherboard represent? It's a larger (longer) timeframe that all the individual single events get plugged into.

Did that make any sense? You got it? Feeling better now? Good. So now that the tech session is over and done with . . . you can go ahead and send three easy payments of $29.95! HA!

The timeline chart in this book is based on pre-existing scriptural, historical, and astronomical data. I did my best to correctly locate all the events. *But only time will tell.*

The moral of the story? God is sovereign over the terrestrial, the celestial, and even time.

I hope you've found this book interesting.

Proverbs 25:2
It is the glory of God to conceal a thing: but the honor of kings is to search out a matter.

We are prompted by God to search for answers. He never said the search was going to be easy.

Addendum

Quick Reference Guide & Notes

The importance of referencing a good concordance to accurately translate the Hebrew and Greek texts cannot be underestimated. It's an essential tool, especially when getting to the core meaning of certain texts that have prophetic implications. And as I found out in the course of doing this research, the accurately translated texts of interest revealed some amazing and very serious information.

I guess that in the early days of the protestant reformation, when the great linguists and translators were bypassing the Latin Vulgate in order to get to the real truth, the newly revealed gems of scripture shined almost as brightly as the transfiguration. What a wonderful thing it must have been to chip away the limestone and find a mother load of gold just beneath!

That's exactly what I experienced when starting down this path of study. I hope that this quick-reference guide will help you to hit on some of the main points that formed the foundation of this book.

Long-Range Time-Frame Template

Part 1: Genesis chapter 1 and 2

Six total days of creation work, and the last day (7th day) dedicated to "rest".

Part 2: 2 Peter 3:8

"But beloved, be not ignorant of this one thing, that one day is with the Lord is as a thousand years, and a thousand years as one day."

This unusual correlation shows a view of the two time frames that are used interchangeably (by God). The location of the 7th day of rest (Sabbath rest) has strong indications to a future 7th one thousand year period of peace under the authority and leadership of God Jesus Christ. The first six thousand years of turmoil and chaos will see a sudden regime change for the better. Also, the location of the infamous number 7, in terms of chronology, seems to be very strategic in it's placement here.

This design is commonly understood among Biblical scholars as not only the original creation period but as a structure or template for a long-term timeline.

This long-term concept breaks down as follows:

Phase 1:

The human world system operates for a fixed continuous 6000-year (interchanged 6 day) period.

Phase 2:

The entire world system undergoes a permanent

shift to a fixed 1000-year (interchanged 1 day) period.

Why it is that this crossover between short-term and long-term time references is a factor that we must consider is something that I can't quite totally grasp. I can only guess that in God's higher realm, He in His infinite wisdom has ordained it and I'll just have to restrain any speculation. At present, the unknown is resolved by having faith that things will be crystal clear someday in the future, in God's due time. And I have to admit in all honesty that this frankly annoys me. ☺

Calendar—Original Biblical Legacy System

Part 1: Genesis 1:14

> "And God said, Let there be lights in the firmament of the heaven to divide the day from the night; and let them be for signs, and for seasons, and for days, and years."

The English word "seasons" (actual Hebrew word = "mowed" or "moad" or "mowadah") according to Strong's Concordance #4150 has the following definition.

The primary definition that is listed for these three Hebrew words is an "appointment" or "fixed time". This would naturally assume that there's a pre-existing timing structure or calendar system already running in the background. Even today, we commonly mark appointments on a calendar.

Furthermore, the words "days and years" in the verse are unmistakably talking about a calendar system. The broader implication in Gen 1:14 is that this original calendar system is the basis for properly tracking all chronology both past and present. Also, the precise scheduling of God's prophetic events (appointments) would be included in the calendar system.

A more accurate translation of Gen 1:14 would be:

> "And God said, Let there be lights in the firmament of the heaven to divide the day from the night; and let them be for signs, and for appointments, and for days, and years."

Part 2: Genesis 7:11:
> "In the six hundredth year of Noah's life, in the second month, the seventeenth day of the month, the same day…"

Genesis 7 and 8 (Noah's ark) have specific references to months and dates.

The second month = May
The seventeenth day = May 17

The events (historical and prophetic) in the scriptures are detailed to varying degrees and every one of them is set against the timing "backdrop" which is a calendar system authored by God.

Part 3: Genesis 5, 10 and 11:
Very accurate record-keeping for life spans and genealogies at this early stage of human existence is apparent. The entire catalog of information indicates a highly developed sense of organization and structure. A method for charting the advancement of lineage would naturally require a calendar system.

This calendar system is the original Biblical legacy calendar system, which is primarily based on lunar cycles and preceded the later developed Julian-Gregorian calendar system, which is primarily solar based. As is so often the case, the latter is a compromised distortion, which tends to fuzzy up the truth.

Astronomical Signs Or Signals

Genesis 1:14
> "And God said, Let there be lights in the firmament of the heaven to divide the day from the night; and let them be for signs, and for seasons, and for days, and years."

The English word "seasons" (actual Hebrew word = "owth") according to Strong's Concordance #226 has the following definition.

The primary definition that is listed for this word is "signal" (as in the appearance of a signal). Also listed are the words "flag" and "beacon". These are definitely meant as attention grabbing devices. There's no other plausible explanation.

The words "seasons" is ambiguous and doesn't really make for a good match as far as the context of the verse is concerned. It's kind of like finding a speed bump in the middle of a racetrack. It just doesn't make very good sense.

An even more accurate and complete translation of Gen 1:14, including the word "appointments" from the calendar section, would be:

> "And God said, Let there be lights in the firmament of the heaven to divide the day from the night; and let them be for signals, and for appointments, and for days, and years."

The words "lights in the firmament of the heavens" includes the sun, moon and stars, which are all in the celestial catalog.

The conclusion that has to be reached as a result of this more accurate translation is that God will be "SIGNALING" (sending signals) to us by using the sun, moon and stars. The signals would naturally have to be in the form that is recognizable to us. And that would mean eclipses, conjunctions, alignments and constellation-based configurations which are all observable from ground-level terra firma with naked eye vision.

Furthermore, given the highly organized format that God has ordained for His celestial storyboard media, it stands to reason that the signals would be strategically appointed within His calendar system. Thus the Star of Bethlehem DVD study has a lot of merit in bearing this out. Kudos to Rick Larson! We've now got a green light to explore some star charts.

The Celestial Signal in Revelation 12

Revelation 12:1

> "And there appeared a great wonder in heaven; a woman clothed with the sun, and the moon under her feet, and upon her head a crown of twelve stars":

Let's tackle this one in the exact same way that was done with the other scriptures.

The English word "wonder" (actual Greek word = "semeion") according to Strong's Concordance #4592 has the following definition.

The primary definitions that are listed for this word are "miracle", "sign", "token" and "wonder".

An even more accurate and complete translation of Rev 12:1 would be:

> "And there appeared a miraculous star-based signal in heaven; a woman clothed with the sun, and the moon under her feet, and upon her head a crown of twelve stars":

It's clear that the weightier definitions in this case speak of a miraculous sign (signal) or token (symbol, indication or gesture). I'm not sure why the King James translators and editors chose to use the least significant (vague) word of "wonder". As far as I'm concerned, they blew it. This verse should not have been subjected to theatrical whims. The main intention in this part of the verse is to issue or convey a very strong signal in the form of a visually apparent celestial configuration. This text is screaming at us to look up into the sky and pay attention! And as the signal is located in heaven, the correlation to a dual-constellation appearance is perfectly suitable.

Question: So what about all the inhabitants on the planet Earth that weren't standing outside their homes, staring up into the sky on September 23rd, 2017, when this important celestial signal was sent? Are they excluded from this new knowledge?

Answer: Fortunately, they're living in a modern era where the ability to learn about this phenomena (past tense) is readily available via web and print media. It's easily available for them. But it would certainly help if they were inclined towards investigating end-times news.

The Virgo–Leo Celestial Lineup

Revelation 12:1
> "And there appeared a miraculous star-based signal in heaven; a woman clothed with the sun, and the moon under her feet, and upon her head a crown of twelve stars."

The twelve stars. What's the significance here?

Well, for starters, the crown (LEO) is the home one particular star that exemplifies the royal stature that relates to someone with royal or regal quality. Thus the name Regulus is the name for this unique star. Regulus in this situation is THE BOSS. For more information on the actual root history behind this naming convention we'd probably have to consult someone like Enoch or perhaps even Adam himself. But the traditional lore with respect to Regulus (and its alternate names) has always ascribed royal status to this particular star.

It can be safely understood that in the standard configuration of Virgo with Leo directly overhead, Leo is assigning Virgo a highly elevated status. If you're somewhat familiar with protocols relevant to traditional Royalty, the person of Royal stature or heritage enjoys a position whereby the subjects who are considered to be under the authority of the Royal personage, actually line up to greet them. And typically this is done at a time that is appointed to them by the Royal scheduler of events.

The constellation Leo (on September 23rd, 2017), in an extremely rare occurrence, had an additional 3 planets fall in line with Regulus. These 3 planets actually lined up below (at the bottom) of the constellation and formed a line that pointed to Regulus and formed the grouping of 12 stars. This almost seems to symbolize a sort of salutation by the 3 local planets (Mercury, Mars and Venus—all in our solar system) to a distant Royal star, Regulus, in an orderly (respectful or compliant) pattern.

The number 12 in this case also hails to the twelve tribes of Israel. This same distinction and prominence is written about in Rev 21:14 pertaining to the new city of

Jerusalem.

Rev 21:12
> And had a wall great and high, and had twelve gates, and at the gates twelve angels, and names written thereon, which are the names of the twelve tribes of the children of Israel.

Rev 21:14
> And the wall of the city had twelve foundations, and in them the names of the twelve apostles of the Lamb.

And of course the Lamb (Jesus Christ) is Royalty from both His Royal heavenly throne as God the Son and also from His Royal pedigree out of the nation Israel.

The Value of a Timeline
This section will be brief.

There's an indwelling consciousness of God in humans that was placed there by God.

This internal awareness of God has with it some extra open circuits that connect to other things such as the knowledge that God's patience has a limit.

Now for the "limit" part.

The long-range time frame as shown in this book speaks to God's limit. It brings into play the typologies, historically accurate chronology, historical background, technical perspective and prophetic astronomy that in my opinion, present a fairly convincing argument for the 7000-year plan and the shorter 7-year plan otherwise known as Daniels 70th week. The 70th week is analyzed further into sub-components that do have accurate correlations to prophetic astronomically oriented texts and applicable typologies.

If the hard facts (data) don't grab ya, I don't know what will.

The Value of a Signal
Matthew 24:37-39

> 37: But as the days of Noah were, so shall also the coming of the Son of man be.
> 38: For as in the days that were before the flood they were eating and drinking, marrying and giving in marriage, until the day that Noah entered into the ark,
> 39: And knew not until the flood came, and took them all away; so shall the coming of the Son of man be.

It will be quite a surprise for those who won't wake up and pay close attention to the signs of the times.

In the days of Noah, there were possibly millions to many millions or more people living on the earth. Noah's ark-boat building project lasted an entire year in which time he preached to anyone and everyone who would listen. Many listened and no doubt relayed Noah's story to others who in turn, did the same. The word was out.

The ark actually served as a warning or signal. But the signal only had value up until the minute that it started raining. A small group of 8 people (Noah and his family) comprised a very small percentage in comparison to the existing standing population at the time. I'm guessing that the flood (likened unto the rapture) left approximately 99% of the living population behind.

But God has indeed signaled to us clearly. It's definitely worth taking note of, regarding as valuable, watching diligently and praying earnestly.

After all, Noah did. And it paid off.

www.ingramcontent.com/pod-product-compliance
Lightning Source LLC
Chambersburg PA
CBHW030905080526
44589CB00010B/152